The Cubbies Fan Word Search

Puzzle Book

The Cubbies Fan Word Search

Puzzle Book

Puzzles by Michael Norton

Reedy Press, PO Box 5131, St. Louis, MO 63139, USA

Library of Congress Control Number: on file

ISBN: 978-1-933370-74-3

puzzles by Michael Norton
cover by Kevin Belford

For information on all Reedy Press publications visit our website at www.reedypress.com.

Printed in the United States of America
08 09 10 11 12 5 4 3 2 1

Batter Up!

GENE HISER
AL BIRDWELL
DENVER GRIGSBY
BERNIE FRIBERG
JOHN HERRNSTEIN
ART WILSON
JOHNNY BATES
THAD BOSLEY
ELMER YOTER
NATE OLIVER

Introducing the Newly-named Cubs

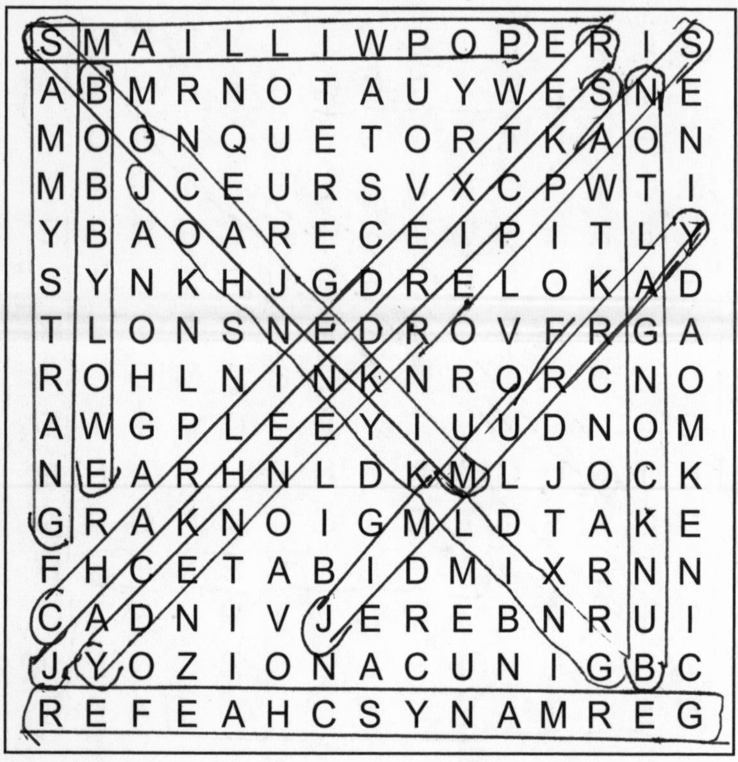

GERMANY SCHAEFER
SAMMY STRANG
BUNK CONGALTON
SNAPPER KENNEDY
JACK HENDRICKS
POP WILLIAMS
JOHNNY KLING
MIKE JACOBS
CHARLIE DEXTER
ED GLENN
BOBBY LOWE
JIM MURRAY

Pitchers

```
R A U T R I C K S E R U F I N
E E A D O S N E D G A R V I N
U L G A L Y T O O M E K A J A
A L O R O C K C L D O N D I M
E E U J E T I N R A G R I P E
S S U L I B O U M N A K D I L
S S P M O S S O I K T I R B O
A U Y A I S P N C B Y G O E C
P R I L E R N A E R W A B W E
E K S L L I P A E F O E H C O
D C L M T E C Y E R F O C A J
U A I D N T K E A C S A I L D
A J U E R A T B O R E C R E G
L B G R A Y T O O N A R A K L
C N R O B S O B O B T I S A K
```

GENE PACKARD
JACK RUSSELL
RICH BORDI
CLAUDE PASSEAU
BOB OSBORN
K. (KEN) RAFFENSBERGER
NED GARVIN
BUD TINNING
RAY PRIM
BOB KELLY
JOE COLEMAN
JAKE MOOTY

Outfielders

```
T A H A C K M I L L E R M E N
L N O A P E T E R A X E A N H
A Q A O R I S B N O T O O W I
H C U N N R A D K I R T E V G
J Y H A E H Y F I E N R I E J
M O L U M S A W U R D Y O R P
Y O E K C P I G O H P R O E N
L R A C Y K I H E L G S T L E
L U E D A F T A W E T E C L T
E V N I S R T A A E S E W A Y
K A E U E E T L N C T B R W E
E C S T M A T E O N O E R E O
O E L Y O M T T R R E A P Y D
J A A D A E T A F U G R O T K
W R T N P T O M L I W T L A W
```

PETE WHISENANT
HARRY WOLTER
JOE KELLY
ANDY PAFKO
JESUS FIGUEROA
WALTER THORNTON
WALT WILMOT
HACK MILLER
PETE SCOTT
GEORGE ALTMAN
CHUCK TANNER
JOE CARTER
TYE WALLER

On the Mound

```
E D O W N I E G O N D U L P H
B A Z E B D O C C S S Y O V Z
R O N M A H A Y U I M C J E D
E F B W O G A M T I L K D I N
P O N L M R L R K A L N C A O
S E T H O A U E U I A K S I T
B A X I C C H L P N I N A V P
O C T K K A K P R E C I C K M
D R C C R A S E U H F I T E O
G I A K L T H O R N U M Y A C
D J E O E N R A O Y H T E R T
N Y E I O C T A K Y O O D O N
A C N M I B U T O L D U J I I
R E A N P O S O L H I C A T L
T R I E O P E C L O M U R E C
```

CLINT COMPTON	BOB LOCKER
DICK CALMUS	JOHN UPHAM
RAMON HERNANDEZ	JACK CURTIS
BEN WADE	RON MAHAY
J. (JOHNNY) KLIPPSTEIN	MIKE HARKEY

Just More Diamond Dudes

A	S	U	O	H	C	E	P	E	I	L	R	A	H	C
R	I	L	L	E	W	X	A	M	N	O	S	A	J	E
T	E	N	O	P	U	C	K	I	L	S	O	A	Y	R
I	T	G	A	M	E	R	I	T	E	L	T	O	H	I
S	C	O	N	E	R	I	G	N	C	T	O	A	D	U
T	O	F	M	I	O	A	O	J	O	E	R	A	Y	G
W	E	I	H	M	Z	J	M	I	T	R	O	E	B	A
A	U	D	D	O	Y	T	C	S	Y	P	A	I	C	M
N	I	D	K	C	I	S	N	W	O	R	L	R	U	E
E	U	C	R	E	I	T	E	U	L	L	N	O	N	I
S	T	E	V	P	A	A	Z	W	H	O	R	T	I	D
T	P	O	C	U	V	R	E	E	E	T	D	A	Y	D
E	B	R	O	E	C	B	N	I	T	L	L	A	C	E
B	A	R	R	Y	B	R	O	S	S	E	L	A	T	R
M	S	M	O	K	Y	B	U	R	G	E	S	S	W	F

WALT HUNTZINGER
BILL HENRY
CHARLIE PECHOUS
FREDDIE MAGUIRE
TED KEARNS
MARC PISCIOTTA
TOMMY SEWELL

CARLOS MARMOL
SMOKY BURGESS
HARRY WEAVER
EARL WEBB
JASON MAXWELL
PERCY JONES

Warming Up

D	R	E	T	B	I	L	L	H	A	N	D	S	N	J
T	O	W	L	Y	A	C	I	V	U	A	D	O	O	A
O	L	F	A	H	L	E	K	O	T	M	S	N	D	C
N	L	A	M	I	S	T	R	I	I	R	P	K	O	S
E	O	P	A	U	L	T	O	L	E	E	V	H	N	O
T	R	A	S	H	I	K	T	D	R	B	E	E	P	L
N	H	E	N	K	R	W	N	L	I	R	D	T	R	I
O	C	Y	A	D	I	A	M	L	B	E	H	Y	I	N
F	S	A	M	L	S	A	L	H	M	G	L	O	N	E
Y	L	V	C	T	N	Y	U	O	I	E	D	O	C	G
A	A	O	T	K	H	T	T	R	A	G	A	L	E	P
R	X	O	T	O	S	H	W	G	E	R	I	U	M	T
A	C	D	E	O	L	L	I	R	N	O	I	T	M	R
S	E	F	N	Y	E	W	F	U	L	E	Y	R	I	I
H	T	C	E	M	S	T	C	A	R	G	E	B	A	Z

MEL WRIGHT
JON PERLMAN
SCOTT SANDERSON
MILT WILCOX
BILLY HOEFT
GEORGE GERBERMAN
AL SCHROLL
RAY FONTENOT
HERB HUTSON
BILL HANDS
DON PRINCE
TOM EDENS

"Give Me a C!"

Y	A	N	S	E	S	T	I	C	K	B	U	M	O	P
T	I	D	O	U	G	C	A	P	I	L	L	A	B	U
N	O	W	R	A	X	I	T	L	I	K	E	W	I	L
E	N	K	N	E	O	H	L	A	N	O	I	B	T	A
V	E	B	D	I	T	Y	A	E	L	L	I	G	N	R
I	D	E	V	O	C	T	I	B	L	L	E	N	E	R
L	E	A	R	O	N	I	O	C	L	R	U	T	M	Y
O	C	G	W	I	P	C	U	C	A	I	R	U	E	C
T	Y	A	T	N	A	N	A	Y	Y	A	H	A	L	H
E	N	J	U	R	N	M	C	R	C	E	N	I	C	E
M	N	A	X	A	P	U	I	L	D	T	V	E	T	N
U	O	R	N	B	L	A	U	I	N	W	S	R	T	E
W	R	E	E	P	H	A	O	E	B	S	E	T	A	Y
I	D	L	O	T	P	C	U	L	P	O	T	L	M	H
N	L	M	A	H	T	W	I	Z	A	B	O	M	L	I

RONNY CEDENO
WILL CUNNANE
BILLY COWAN
DON CARDWELL
LARRY CHENEY
DOUG CAPILLA

MATT CLEMENT
BILL CAMPBELL
PAUL CARTER
RAY CULP
HARVEY COTTER

Hail To All These Hurlers

R	L	L	E	P	P	O	P	N	A	V	D	D	O	T
F	E	C	W	H	I	P	P	O	V	A	U	G	H	N
A	R	G	S	I	E	T	F	A	Y	N	A	U	R	M
Y	A	A	D	H	L	I	P	S	T	O	R	E	N	P
B	L	R	Z	I	L	B	H	T	O	R	D	K	V	I
L	P	R	A	N	R	E	U	W	A	N	I	T	C	P
A	E	I	O	E	O	D	R	R	E	N	U	C	H	A
R	N	F	Y	U	B	T	N	V	C	E	I	E	K	N
R	H	U	T	J	H	S	A	A	R	O	T	L	C	T
Y	K	K	B	Y	X	L	I	E	T	F	O	T	W	O
G	A	N	E	P	Y	A	I	C	S	S	I	P	H	M
U	P	U	G	M	S	O	J	V	N	M	E	L	E	A
R	O	T	M	A	S	L	R	Z	D	A	O	T	R	R
A	D	I	L	G	O	I	C	K	M	G	R	T	E	D
N	J	A	C	K	A	K	E	R	F	P	A	F	T	P

TODD VAN POPPEL
HIPPO VAUGHN
PETE STANDRIDGE
WILBUR COOPER
JIMMY LAVENDER
JACK AKER
LARRY GURA
TOM SEATON
LEFTY YORK

10

C	I	N	R	E	B	O	D	S	S	E	J	E	D	D
D	N	B	A	S	E	T	A	G	D	U	C	R	L	N
E	T	O	V	I	K	N	R	A	L	E	D	O	M	O
J	C	B	S	N	I	H	W	I	R	I	O	D	D	S
O	A	B	F	N	T	N	Y	I	R	C	I	R	S	N
H	R	Y	E	T	E	A	F	D	V	C	A	O	K	H
N	M	G	B	B	R	H	A	C	K	E	R	B	A	O
N	E	E	E	A	T	M	P	C	B	C	E	U	R	J
Y	N	N	L	S	L	L	U	E	F	U	L	C	T	N
K	M	E	T	A	W	L	V	F	T	O	T	S	I	E
L	A	S	S	G	L	A	E	S	J	S	A	K	M	B
I	U	M	O	E	D	J	D	R	Y	E	L	E	M	I
N	R	I	R	U	R	O	Y	L	E	S	L	I	E	L
G	O	T	I	N	Y	O	S	B	O	R	N	E	H	O
J	U	H	G	F	O	G	R	I	H	H	Y	T	U	P

CARMEN MAURO
BOBBY GENE SMITH
PHIL STEPHENSON
BEN JOHNSON
DAVE BEARD
JESS DOBERNIC
DICK CULLER
JOHNNY KLING
TINY OSBORNE
ROY LESLIE
JAY BALLER
SAL MADRID
BEN WADE
JEFF CROSS

They Wore the Uniform

```
K M S W O R R U B N H O J N E
O W I L L I A M B R E N N A N
D Z A K Z N N U Y J A K E L L
E X E P E E I I Q U E S K E R
Z B A N T C N C V I C R Y E A
O O I O E H A O G E T P A D M
D D E L W M K M D E N I X E O
P S P I L L I H P R O L Y A T
I A O A E F A J I B O M I J E
C U U E U K L V Y T E Y R H A
H T T L G L O E R N W L E I P
A E N F N R B N M E N O L R A
P S T B V O U A D I D A R C R
D O O S F U C B K I N F M M I
T E X C A R L E T O N G I M S
```

JOHN BURROWS	BILL FLEMING
PETE ELKO	PHIL NEVIN
REY ORDONEZ	PAUL NOCE
WILLIAM BRENNAN	PAUL BAKO
TAYLOR PHILLIPS	MANNY JIMENEZ
MIKE CAMPBELL	TEX CARLETON

“Chicago Fire” Ballers

T	A	D	E	G	R	E	G	T	A	M	I	L	S	A
H	E	R	N	I	M	O	T	W	A	N	E	D	E	C
O	S	T	E	V	E	O	N	R	E	G	I	N	Y	L
G	L	U	S	T	R	E	K	I	A	L	E	R	O	A
U	R	Y	R	D	T	P	A	S	G	H	O	N	T	R
T	I	E	K	B	R	U	S	A	T	A	W	N	E	K
C	D	C	G	I	O	O	S	O	D	A	N	F	N	G
I	I	O	O	M	G	B	L	E	R	N	J	D	A	R
D	I	R	O	H	A	G	T	N	C	E	A	N	C	I
O	I	D	C	W	C	D	E	K	N	U	G	H	W	F
D	F	I	O	M	Y	K	D	K	M	A	R	E	E	F
Y	R	O	N	R	E	R	I	U	L	L	I	B	L	I
R	A	N	B	E	D	N	R	E	X	J	O	M	A	T
A	Y	P	A	U	S	O	R	E	S	T	R	U	C	H
L	F	O	G	I	J	A	R	G	K	I	K	C	E	D

LON WARNEKE
BOB RUSH
CLARK GRIFFITH
LYNN MCGLOTHEN
KERRY WOOD
F. (FERGUSON) JENKINS
DICK DROTT
MARK PRIOR
GREG MADDUX
RICH GOSSAGE
BRUCE SUTTER

The El Brought You To These Guys

```
T N S H C I L A E R H H Y P J
O A I S G T M E P A B R D S O
N F Y W O U T M R K A M I K L
O O A O A R O R I E D V S R U
S Y S W G S Y E L K A Y F R A
K T E N A C B O K D E O A P F
C L U S H H Y E M T I C Z O L
A K I I S O S I C F T N U C L
J G T A R A J N L X J A S R I
N I E T V L H Y E W I E M G B
I N O S R E D N E H E V E T S
R G N N A O K N O V Y E O T H
R E O O D N S I E R A O Y M R
A S A L L T H V M N M D R H I
D E R E K B O T E L H O B E T
```

HARRY CHITI
ROY HENSHAW
TROY O'LEARY
DEREK BOTELHO
DARRIN JACKSON
STEVE HENDERSON
DAVEY JOHNSON
JIM DAVIS
MATT KEOUGH
RON HASSEY
MIKE VAIL
BRUCE KIMM
BILL FAUL

Long Throwers From the Warning Track

Y	L	L	A	D	N	A	R	T	W	E	N	A	I	Y
E	E	G	D	G	U	K	V	E	Y	C	O	S	E	H
S	N	U	A	C	A	I	C	E	T	A	T	R	R	I
M	W	T	G	N	O	M	A	R	U	H	N	E	O	J
A	O	L	L	I	H	N	E	L	L	A	N	E	L	G
R	R	S	M	L	R	C	T	K	O	U	B	L	Y	E
O	B	S	I	W	I	L	R	O	N	A	O	D	A	K
D	E	O	M	E	N	G	O	A	X	A	W	I	T	S
N	G	I	N	H	W	O	Y	P	S	B	R	N	Y	E
A	R	F	C	I	O	H	I	N	Y	H	J	F	N	I
N	O	R	U	N	W	S	C	K	N	I	P	O	N	M
R	E	T	A	O	L	O	R	T	E	H	T	D	A	T
E	G	D	R	E	V	I	U	N	U	O	O	C	D	T
F	E	I	T	T	E	D	Y	L	N	B	O	J	H	A
C	R	I	K	C	I	H	C	S	E	I	R	R	O	M

DANNY TAYLOR
GEORGE BROWNE
FERNANDO RAMSEY
GLENALLEN HILL
MORRIE SCHICK
BUTCH WEIS
MATT MIESKE
JOHNNY GILL
NEWT RANDALL
FRANK EMAGA

Pitch & Catch

N	I	V	E	R	E	L	L	I	H	K	N	A	R	F
A	O	P	A	T	M	O	R	A	N	E	K	G	R	D
B	F	S	N	U	P	H	E	R	T	S	O	H	E	L
O	J	N	S	K	I	P	G	U	D	R	A	Y	K	E
C	H	N	O	A	W	O	C	P	R	R	D	I	L	V
N	S	H	R	T	I	G	M	E	R	B	O	N	A	E
A	U	I	R	O	W	H	E	Y	I	S	L	O	W	E
L	L	E	R	T	T	O	C	N	G	I	S	N	E	L
B	L	R	P	A	V	H	T	T	O	C	L	P	B	Y
Y	I	F	R	A	A	J	A	A	T	I	H	E	U	H
R	M	C	R	P	L	F	I	R	Z	O	D	A	R	P
N	E	O	M	M	I	L	O	N	E	E	C	R	M	L
E	L	A	H	S	U	K	L	I	M	E	B	S	C	L
H	N	T	E	P	A	T	M	O	R	E	N	O	S	I
N	E	S	N	A	M	E	N	O	T	S	L	L	I	B

BILL STONEMAN
SCOTT CHIASSON
ENSIGN COTTRELL
EMIL KUSH
FRANK HILLER
BILL PHYLE
HARRY CHAPMAN
HENRY BLANCO
RUBE WALKER
PAT MORAN

They Played With Three Fingers Brown

S	U	B	B	R	O	L	Y	A	T	K	C	A	Z	R
O	Y	N	A	C	T	E	Y	I	W	T	S	O	X	B
O	A	E	D	I	F	U	O	G	O	O	L	J	U	I
E	D	S	N	O	W	H	F	M	L	L	A	D	N	D
T	U	I	E	S	T	R	W	L	I	C	D	C	O	U
D	I	L	R	M	E	A	Y	E	K	Y	B	K	T	T
N	G	T	O	R	L	H	N	M	S	E	S	T	N	C
A	I	E	O	S	O	O	C	C	R	H	P	A	A	H
Z	A	R	H	F	K	C	H	C	A	N	E	Y	T	R
N	B	Y	M	C	A	U	K	D	M	L	T	L	S	U
A	E	A	A	R	L	I	B	N	E	Y	E	O	M	D
V	N	J	T	T	G	A	F	R	A	R	R	R	O	O
E	M	H	Z	H	R	C	K	E	Z	R	F	R	T	L
K	Y	A	T	R	I	E	N	O	B	O	F	I	A	P
I	E	C	Y	S	E	R	N	I	E	G	R	O	T	H

FRANK CORRIDO
FRED HOLMES
SHAD BARRY
JACK MCCARTHY
HARRY MCCHESNEY
DUTCH RUDOLPH
BUDDY SCHULTZ
ERNIE GROTH
TOM STANTON
SOLLY HOFMAN
ZACK TAYLOR
TOM WALSH
IKE VAN ZANDT

Tinker-to-Evers-to-Chance, and Other Infield Combos

```
L T I S F R A N K C H A N C E
B U S E R J O E S J H O V I M
A I Z S O E B O O M T T K D R
S G L B U S V E C N C S U A E
L I K L M K T E R U W R N U G
A K S I M I T O Y O Y D D F N
E I A K N A H I R N Y V E N I
D P T K I T D T A J N A E E R
E X E E E M S L A W E H F I T
I R O R R O E C O D E W O Y S
L J D I N P K I A C N I N J U
R N W H L S J E D B K G D W O
A F O S O H E N O D E N Y D L
H J L N G F R E D M E R K L E
C H U C K W O R T M A N O Y E
```

CHARLIE DEAL
CHUCK WORTMAN
ANDRE THORNTON
RANDY JACKSON
JOHN OSTROWSKI
FRANK CHANCE
JOE TINKER
FRED MERKLE
BILL MADLOCK
EDDIE MIKSIS
EDDIE WAITKUS
JOHNNY EVERS

Everybody Had a Role

E	D	T	S	A	W	E	N	R	T	I	Z	E	N	M
H	C	I	V	O	K	T	E	M	C	E	V	A	E	R
C	O	N	Y	C	H	A	T	R	U	N	H	R	Y	D
S	L	K	I	D	E	C	E	Q	A	A	W	B	R	V
E	B	I	D	A	D	P	R	A	N	I	T	A	W	E
N	O	L	A	H	T	A	L	S	N	O	W	R	A	M
E	B	A	B	O	M	O	E	J	M	N	B	B	M	I
B	W	R	C	S	N	R	A	N	O	J	I	R	L	K
I	I	S	I	A	B	C	E	T	O	L	O	L	I	E
L	L	U	G	R	O	C	S	F	L	D	C	I	N	N
L	L	F	E	B	I	E	G	Y	L	O	A	G	S	H
Y	F	G	S	R	R	T	O	A	S	Y	J	P	H	U
O	O	O	L	P	T	T	O	Y	L	L	I	B	O	B
R	N	E	O	N	T	N	I	V	R	T	S	V	N	B
T	D	I	V	I	E	C	E	R	O	R	U	O	T	S

KEN HUBBS
MERWIN JACOBSON
PRESTON WARD
ROGER BRESNAHAN
C. (CATFISH) METKOVICH
LUIS MARQUEZ
DON EADDY
BILLY OTT
DEL RICE
BOB WILL

Infielders

```
M I L D A V E O W E N E D O N
A L C H A T O S J E D A I K G
R O E R A N A T U C R O I O O
T I L D N K R F Y T A G G I Z
Y E T L D O I O P U B I A B R
K E R L E I S H H R A H S O E
R O N R E S E Y A N A T O B H
U V I C Y L O M T T U R J B K
G A C U A Z Y R U E C R E Y C
E F O N I X E O E L K H R M U
Z E B T E R R Y D V L I N O B
M A T H E W A X A M A I M R U
A S B O R I A L A N I D G G R
C O N G E H T A W E T J E A O
E A R L O T E B O W O D E N N
```

MIKE TYSON
JIM DOYLE
BUCK HERZOG
EDDIE MULLIGAN
MARTY KRUG
DAVE OWEN
ZEB TERRY
ART PHELAN
DAVE ROSELLO
DAN ROHN
BOBBY MORGAN

They Roared In the 1920s

E	T	S	K	N	A	B	U	E	L	E	U	G	R	N
O	T	T	A	T	R	U	T	Y	G	O	A	I	V	O
N	U	O	R	N	O	T	S	S	O	B	P	M	O	N
S	Y	R	C	E	G	O	F	L	B	W	M	Z	O	N
I	F	M	E	H	N	M	R	Y	H	I	K	L	D	A
S	U	J	R	H	T	I	H	E	R	C	L	A	V	H
A	E	A	Y	D	E	A	E	G	I	I	O	I	F	S
H	J	M	W	W	R	L	E	W	E	L	N	R	U	D
K	S	C	I	T	E	I	L	H	Y	E	R	P	O	E
O	I	U	N	R	L	I	A	E	F	T	E	A	K	R
C	L	E	B	R	G	N	B	B	K	F	F	T	H	J
E	T	I	A	Y	S	Y	X	S	Y	N	I	E	U	C
T	L	H	M	O	U	H	A	H	P	E	H	L	L	V
P	C	A	N	E	U	G	Z	R	O	D	U	O	C	A
S	N	D	A	R	G	E	P	W	A	L	A	B	J	Y

OLLIE HANSON
UEL EUBANKS
GABBY HARTNETT
CHARLIE GRIMM
CLIFF HEATHCOTE
CHARLIE ROOT
JOHN KELLEHER
RAY GRIMES
GUY BUSH
RIP WHEELER
RED SHANNON
LEFTY WEINERT

What Kind Of Name Was That?

```
R H S A R O T T O B S G L T S
E A H T E M U S D L E O R E R
D H C T A B O X E I N N M B B
I O E A O K N F B G O A E U F
E F N W I P T R T I J Z T H E
Z C O D O Y S O S Y O T N G E
N E T C G L M Y E A O U T I F
O I O O C T K X M N R W A N E
I C O Y H L I N S A A O C R N
N D N O I N Y B I Z G T H L E
U E M N V O R I U L N O I A M
B A G S D I L Y B E A H O S K
S L I W G E C O R R K A R N C
E T S G A M E M A T I R I S O
R P S H O R T Y S L A G L E J
```

BUTTONS BRIGGS
TOPSY MAGOON
LONG TOM THOMAS
JOCK MENEFEE
KANGAROO JONES
NIXEY JAMES
LINK LOWE
NOISY KLING
LEFTY GOOD
SHORTY SLAGLE

Friends Of the Ivy

E	T	H	A	N	A	L	L	E	N	I	D	E	T	N
H	M	O	L	A	N	A	D	B	O	C	F	R	O	A
R	G	A	O	K	H	I	J	O	E	Y	E	D	N	H
A	I	D	R	K	R	F	C	C	A	B	N	D	O	G
E	F	M	Y	V	N	A	N	O	L	E	Y	L	U	A
H	O	V	E	L	R	A	L	I	L	P	I	O	N	L
Y	A	I	M	R	L	I	G	C	A	G	L	U	U	L
M	S	Y	L	D	E	E	C	F	E	A	P	G	P	A
M	E	A	A	C	I	M	K	K	S	V	B	U	T	C
A	T	Z	K	L	D	O	K	E	E	C	A	R	A	Y
S	I	Z	R	Y	E	T	S	C	O	R	H	D	B	T
C	Y	A	O	E	J	I	O	S	R	J	T	W	O	R
E	H	L	X	E	O	L	N	Y	H	O	J	A	S	A
C	L	O	U	M	T	O	D	E	L	H	I	A	S	M
P	E	A	N	U	T	S	L	O	W	R	E	Y	U	G

PEANUTS LOWREY
LLOYD MCCLENDON
ETHAN ALLEN
MARTY CALLAGHAN
MARV RICKERT
ANDY PAFKO
DAVE CLARK
JOE KELLY
CHARLIE GILBERT
MOISES ALOU

More Lakeside Lads

N	O	D	E	I	W	O	B	H	A	C	I	M	E	W
H	U	F	A	S	K	I	P	H	U	D	E	A	N	E
W	O	L	T	N	E	C	S	I	R	L	K	B	I	R
S	R	R	L	I	R	L	I	A	T	U	R	C	A	E
M	D	K	A	Y	D	O	W	M	E	I	A	K	R	K
A	J	E	E	C	M	S	H	A	A	D	E	N	R	R
I	C	I	C	E	I	C	F	N	P	E	E	N	O	A
L	M	N	T	R	R	O	M	B	R	V	I	U	L	B
L	A	R	H	A	N	C	P	C	G	I	H	D	W	E
I	R	C	S	I	N	A	G	I	A	C	C	N	E	I
W	T	A	S	I	F	U	S	U	N	T	I	O	R	H
T	I	E	C	O	O	T	O	N	O	A	R	R	D	C
R	N	H	R	D	O	H	L	A	C	D	A	N	N	I
A	O	I	N	I	F	A	R	E	S	N	A	D	A	R
L	O	N	O	S	P	M	O	H	T	T	T	O	C	S

ANDREW LORRAINE
DAN SERAFINI
MICAH BOWIE
SCOTT THOMPSON
HORACIO PINA
CHRIS WARD
ART WILLIAMS
BRIAN MCNICHOL
RICHIE BARKER
DOUG CREEK
J. C. MARTIN
RON DUNN
DAN ROHN

Pitch & Catch

D	R	E	T	T	O	C	K	C	I	D	O	C	K	T
T	N	P	R	Y	E	R	R	I	Z	O	V	U	I	T
S	P	A	W	E	A	F	E	Y	F	F	M	T	O	R
A	C	T	M	V	L	O	G	O	Z	B	E	Y	R	A
R	A	M	P	P	C	L	N	G	L	B	I	J	O	N
E	P	O	B	I	A	R	I	M	O	D	N	N	S	T
C	A	R	O	T	B	H	H	H	R	H	E	I	V	E
A	U	A	K	E	E	A	C	E	K	W	D	H	E	R
W	L	N	U	N	V	A	E	Y	O	N	S	L	S	A
R	M	D	U	O	F	N	H	Y	R	U	A	M	A	V
O	I	E	C	G	G	H	E	X	K	R	S	R	L	E
G	N	T	E	T	B	K	K	L	I	D	A	L	F	C
G	N	O	I	L	C	N	I	R	O	H	N	H	A	O
A	E	S	D	I	N	M	M	S	U	L	T	C	M	U
J	R	O	M	R	E	E	Z	T	I	Y	R	B	O	S

MIKE HECHINGER
HARRY CHAPMAN
EMIL KUSH
DICK COTTER
FRANK HILLER
MICKEY OWEN
PAUL MINNER

Look For These Leftys

```
R T O D A E H E R O M H T E S
M O H H I X T I N T Y W A R S
E O N L C L O W E R O B S K O
L L R B L N D R I X A T J I M
A K L R I S E D I T R O K J L
F C A A I L A R R E E Z A E A
F A R N R E L A F H E K Y H M
E M T A B P S F A Y E B O W H
A L I N G R E T O W R R D M E
M L C H A L T I E X K R A O R
O I I U G E R I L E E I A T A
B B G I N U M O B L V N D L L
O L A N A E T U B O I E N A L
C R P T R O R A N D Y W N E E
C I G N I L W O D E V A D S K
```

CRAIG LEFFERTS	BILL FOXEN
JAKE WEIMER	RUBE KROH
BILL MACK	SETH MOREHEAD
MORRIE STEEVENS	JOE HATTEN
DAVE DOWLING	LARRY FRENCH
MAL MOSS	WILLIE PRALL

Hey Batter, Hey Batter ...

G	N	I	T	A	E	K	K	C	I	H	C	J	E	O
Y	T	E	S	A	R	U	Q	U	P	V	I	N	C	R
A	Y	W	E	K	F	Y	B	H	D	M	L	E	H	A
T	T	L	W	S	K	U	A	B	A	Z	E	K	L	Z
G	R	W	F	S	L	L	O	S	S	K	C	O	I	Z
N	A	E	B	A	T	L	B	N	C	I	U	M	T	I
A	W	P	L	O	L	E	A	I	S	J	C	N	J	N
M	E	R	D	L	L	H	P	U	O	M	A	O	D	N
D	T	D	O	L	E	E	C	H	Q	Y	X	D	A	A
U	S	K	J	A	I	K	N	S	E	M	T	U	E	C
A	Y	O	N	D	C	S	K	G	Y	N	I	F	M	S
R	F	V	D	A	O	I	R	N	C	R	S	J	U	I
B	F	E	J	N	H	O	O	J	A	N	R	O	K	R
O	U	G	O	L	E	G	A	L	M	R	P	A	N	H
B	T	T	S	G	O	E	F	I	C	I	F	R	L	C

LARRY SCHLAFLY
GEORGE YANTZ
JIM QUALLS
JACK CUSICK
JIM ASBELL
CHRIS CANNIZZARO
W. (WALTER) STEPHENSON
TUFFY STEWART
BOB RAUDMAN
FRANK KELLERT
CHICK KEATING
LOU JOHNSON
AL TODD

Who's On Deck?

```
T Z E N I T R A M E V A D O L
T A C H U P E D S I R D O L N
O B N A N R E K R U B O E L E
I I O D S E E Y N K A W S B M
R L T P R W D Z T N K E S N Y
R L S R H A I D Y C E P V H H
A N G E W I L D A R O W E U E
M O N A G I L L U M E I D D E
M B I T N H B D I B N V S T L
A O V E J M E T O D T E M I T
I L I M I U R C E U E S L O H
L D L T R Y I B T C G V F R T
L I M A T M R A E D H L E O L
I G C O G T C O N G E R A T S
W T A L T O M G R A N T T S S
```

PHIL DOUGLAS
LEN MADDEN
EDDIE MULLIGAN
WILLIAM MARRIOTT
DAVE MARTINEZ
M. (MICKEY) LIVINGSTON
TIM BLACKWELL
TOM VERYZER
TOM GRANT
LEO BURKE
STEVE DILLARD

The Wind Up, and the Pitch

F	E	R	C	H	I	C	K	F	R	A	S	E	R	N
R	R	H	J	O	E	L	Y	T	A	V	O	L	T	U
E	O	A	D	A	S	K	C	A	J	N	R	X	N	R
D	O	K	N	S	C	O	P	I	E	E	Y	A	C	O
K	M	E	C	K	I	K	M	D	V	E	M	I	O	T
E	L	K	Y	N	M	W	D	A	N	E	O	B	T	E
N	R	A	N	E	E	O	E	O	G	R	D	I	E	L
C	A	O	R	A	N	W	R	A	S	O	L	J	N	S
R	E	V	V	N	E	O	H	R	O	C	O	A	B	N
O	G	E	E	I	M	Y	T	C	I	K	H	M	O	I
S	R	L	L	M	E	F	D	D	S	S	G	E	B	W
B	L	R	I	S	A	N	C	E	E	Y	S	L	R	O
Y	O	J	A	S	Y	D	N	A	R	R	D	E	N	D
T	I	C	U	M	B	E	R	L	A	F	F	U	Y	I
S	A	M	O	H	T	O	M	D	E	T	T	O	R	E

ED DONNELLY
TOM DETTORE
JIM MORONEY
CASEY HAGEMAN
FRED TONEY
RUDY SCHWENCK
FRANK MORRISSEY
JIM WEAVER
KEN CROSBY
EARL MOORE
ORLIE WEAVER
CHICK FRASER
JACK DOSCHER

Donning the Apparel

Y	D	D	N	L	L	E	W	D	R	A	C	N	O	D
N	O	D	X	E	A	L	E	T	N	O	D	E	W	O
N	N	A	R	N	S	R	E	M	M	I	Z	N	O	D
T	B	E	L	E	L	R	V	P	C	L	N	O	D	O
R	R	O	S	H	G	I	A	A	G	O	D	R	D	M
A	Y	D	I	L	A	N	S	L	S	O	A	B	U	T
B	A	O	D	R	R	E	I	T	N	N	S	R	L	D
E	N	A	U	O	L	A	R	S	O	O	D	T	O	L
T	T	R	K	P	N	E	C	E	S	N	D	N	F	E
T	N	S	N	I	B	H	L	N	A	E	Y	F	L	N
O	O	O	F	O	U	N	U	L	O	O	K	C	O	K
N	D	E	R	L	O	E	N	R	U	D	I	N	D	N
N	S	N	Z	D	N	O	D	N	S	J	C	I	O	O
O	O	E	Z	M	D	O	G	N	O	T	L	S	T	D
D	O	N	A	L	D	A	T	V	E	H	E	D	R	S

DON CARDWELL
DON LEONARD
DON KESSINGER
DON BRYANT
DON ROBERTSON
DON NOTTEBART

DON ZIMMER
DON HURST
DON CARLSEN
DON SCHULZE
DON LARSEN
DON YOUNG

Take Me Out To a Ballgame

O	Z	E	U	G	I	N	O	J	E	R	R	S	Y	A
J	B	T	A	L	O	M	I	W	E	L	G	O	L	N
I	X	I	R	I	F	M	O	K	R	N	D	B	K	D
M	N	S	T	U	K	U	C	U	I	E	E	I	G	Y
B	Y	E	N	I	T	I	Z	N	S	N	T	R	A	L
U	H	T	R	O	W	S	N	R	A	F	E	L	Y	K
L	I	B	R	B	M	E	N	I	O	G	O	R	L	A
L	Y	O	O	A	J	M	S	O	H	A	O	L	D	G
I	T	B	S	N	M	A	I	I	Y	G	A	F	A	R
N	E	O	I	S	C	E	B	T	N	N	D	A	N	A
G	R	B	L	Y	S	B	O	H	E	R	A	L	N	V
E	O	T	R	H	A	Y	O	J	I	I	R	T	Y	Y
R	O	R	I	R	B	J	O	C	K	V	Z	O	S	D
I	A	J	D	H	W	L	L	I	G	C	T	Z	T	N
L	E	N	O	L	I	D	L	E	U	G	I	M	O	A

MIGUEL DILONE
JOHN GORYL
KYLE FARNSWORTH
LARRY CASIAN
GREG HIBBARD
ROBIN JENNINGS
ANDY VARGA
JOE MARTY
BOB WICKER
JIM KIRBY
TANYON STURTZ
OZZIE TIMMONS
JIM BULLINGER

More Of the Guys

```
T E M P D O R B O H A G N E R
I J I J O H A R A O A S W I O
M N A D E P T L Z R O R Y E L
O X O S D B B I R C E E K K Y
N O E S O R I Y A B N D E E A
A Y O R E N J L I O A S N V T
S E A E O E H E L V B O D I Y
T G D W S O L A E L L U M N M
A E U T W K M G R A E L G F M
N O A E N Y U T M D H E B O A
O D V A L M A Y T I T C E S S
T R H L P Y L S O O J K Y T A
E L I E U L S E M L C R E E P
K B R A I N C O U L T S I R A
Y T P B S E R E V Y D N A R T
```

GARRY JESTADT
BILLY MALONEY
KEVIN FOSTER
HAL BREEDEN
DAVE GUMPERT
SAMMY TAYLOR
RANDY VERES

BILL LEE
JIM GLEESON
CAL HOWE
SCOTT MOORE
HANK LEIBER
JASON HARDTKE

Sure . . . But Can He Hit a Curve?

E	T	L	U	H	C	S	K	N	A	R	F	W	P	E
H	D	A	T	W	E	L	C	H	S	O	N	L	R	P
P	P	O	T	L	J	I	T	H	E	R	E	Y	U	P
A	S	L	M	W	H	O	A	M	I	S	E	A	H	A
R	R	I	O	I	M	E	S	D	R	O	O	L	O	P
I	T	U	R	D	N	R	A	E	H	N	D	U	U	L
G	O	F	A	R	U	G	F	M	M	K	T	V	S	E
S	C	L	H	E	A	R	O	N	N	O	C	M	I	J
U	Y	N	N	T	C	H	N	R	W	O	L	F	F	R
K	R	I	C	O	M	O	C	E	A	F	O	I	N	U
E	P	P	A	T	D	E	T	I	K	M	S	E	N	L
Y	I	R	O	J	D	E	R	F	V	H	O	F	E	A
Y	E	R	F	Y	N	N	O	L	A	K	I	S	T	H
H	C	A	R	M	E	N	F	A	N	Z	O	N	E	R
W	U	D	O	N	T	E	W	I	L	L	I	S	H	Y

JOSE MOLINA
LONNY FREY
CARMEN FANZONE
KEN RUDOLPH
VIC HARRIS
JIM CONNOR
FRANK SCHULTE
TOM DALY
TED TAPPE
DOMINGO RAMOS

Now . . . Pinch Hitting

N P J E S I T O W I L L Y L L
A Y A E R P O B E N A Y O L A
M R A O R I I F U G Y N L R L
R H T D W R C E I G N E U E L
E C X T N M Y H M I B I F B E
M I H N E O U K B S O J U R B
M V C P O R M F I O P Z G U A
I O K H O K R K A N R A L S C
Z P N R B E N A C O D D T S C
E O R U Y A L D B I H A I E O
I P T N R E R S O O R W L L B
N L Z F V F S R L X B J K L N
I U A V U D E H Y B I M C O H
E A J A C K M C N O T H U B O
H P E N W O R B N O R Y B J J

HEINIE ZIMMERMAN
FRANK ISBELL
JOHN BOCCABELLA
PAUL POPOVICH
RICK MONDAY
RICH BORDI
JUMBO BARRETT
JERRY KINDALL
BYRON BROWNE

Al Capone Watched These Guys Play

L	S	N	A	M	R	E	H	Y	L	L	I	B	M	N
G	E	E	R	J	A	C	E	D	E	G	A	R	I	O
A	R	S	M	O	O	N	E	D	W	I	L	R	K	S
N	P	U	S	I	M	H	B	I	V	L	O	K	E	O
O	N	P	O	W	R	A	N	E	T	L	E	K	K	B
R	O	A	R	B	E	G	N	N	Y	D	R	O	R	O
U	I	C	M	C	H	E	H	A	Y	E	K	L	E	B
J	V	A	H	R	C	C	T	G	Y	W	O	A	E	S
I	A	T	D	I	E	Y	I	L	I	E	E	N	V	M
N	C	K	K	A	R	H	L	R	A	E	S	L	I	I
A	S	T	I	R	Y	O	Y	T	E	N	L	Y	C	T
R	S	X	A	E	R	M	G	O	I	C	D	R	H	H
U	A	H	S	R	M	U	M	O	R	A	N	D	U	R
P	H	A	A	R	J	A	C	I	K	E	M	A	T	B
B	R	C	I	L	N	O	Y	R	J	I	L	O	L	O

BURLEIGH GRIMES
CARROLL YERKES
LANCE RICHBOURG
ED BAECHT
LES SWEETLAND
JIMMY ADAIR
LEROY HEERMANN
HARRY TAYLOR
BILLY HERMAN
BOB SMITH
JAKIE MAY
JOHNNY WELCH
MIKE KREEVICH

Basically Benchwarmers

R	A	Y	N	A	X	O	X	T	T	I	C	O	M	T
E	J	I	M	C	O	O	K	O	U	A	D	A	N	E
B	L	H	B	H	N	R	M	D	L	S	N	O	J	F
U	B	I	D	N	A	M	E	E	O	D	M	R	G	L
N	M	O	E	N	Y	L	C	M	Y	U	E	I	L	S
C	A	L	B	R	A	K	L	B	A	M	R	E	P	R
O	D	E	A	B	S	R	R	E	Y	L	B	F	E	T
E	B	U	H	M	A	O	B	L	A	P	E	H	U	R
D	B	E	I	S	O	R	C	E	M	T	U	T	Q	A
L	S	T	K	K	E	S	R	A	L	L	H	A	E	S
E	H	U	S	G	I	V	C	E	F	L	L	E	N	P
L	M	C	N	T	Y	N	A	N	T	A	I	R	R	O
C	O	I	O	B	I	K	H	D	G	T	R	H	O	S
H	G	N	I	V	L	O	G	T	L	A	W	I	E	T
I	T	R	E	R	H	U	L	F	N	H	O	J	A	R

R. E. HILLEBRAND
TOMMY RAUB
ALECK SMITH
BOB BARRETT
GINGER BEAUMONT
OTIS CLYMER
HAL LEATHERS
MANDY BROOKS
PETE LAMER
JIM COOK
VIN CAMPBELL
DAVE SHEAN
ED LENNOX
JOHN FLUHRER
WALT GOLVIN

Bet They Played When They Were Young ... Just Like You

N	E	L	E	S	E	E	R	F	E	G	R	O	E	M
O	T	S	W	S	D	R	A	W	D	E	K	N	A	H
S	I	T	O	M	N	E	E	D	H	A	M	H	V	J
T	M	R	A	D	I	F	O	C	L	J	T	E	O	A
R	H	O	C	C	L	T	R	U	O	O	S	H	N	S
E	O	L	K	O	H	A	M	E	B	E	N	A	R	T
B	S	L	P	D	Y	R	W	N	E	N	S	Y	O	E
O	L	E	E	M	I	A	I	R	Y	A	H	M	S	R
R	E	V	M	V	L	G	F	S	E	I	C	O	R	S
L	Y	I	T	L	G	E	T	Y	K	T	G	E	W	O
Y	J	T	I	I	G	E	K	R	A	R	T	U	D	N
R	X	S	H	R	W	R	D	A	B	A	U	I	L	K
A	Y	V	O	A	E	G	U	C	U	L	N	G	M	O
D	R	E	R	J	E	D	I	D	A	H	E	D	L	G
I	G	T	Y	K	S	V	O	N	Z	O	R	C	I	V

TIM HOSLEY
JOHNNY STEWART
CHRIS KRUG
IRV HIGGINBOTHAM
DARYL ROBERTSON
G. (GEORGE) MITTERWALD
JOE WALLIS
VIC ROZNOVSKY
TOM NEEDHAM
HANK EDWARDS
JIMMY ARCHER
GEORGE FREESE

Stylin'

R	T	F	X	H	A	N	K	O	T	A	D	B	E	E
A	D	E	I	G	L	O	T	E	D	K	C	I	R	B
Y	F	R	N	U	T	T	E	B	O	R	D	D	I	U
T	Y	N	O	O	A	D	I	C	P	O	E	L	N	L
E	E	A	U	L	R	H	W	Y	L	P	L	E	O	L
V	L	N	M	L	E	G	O	N	E	B	H	I	S	E
E	D	D	I	U	K	D	I	G	O	R	K	L	S	D
S	N	O	L	C	I	T	R	N	T	R	V	T	E	W
T	U	R	A	C	E	O	H	H	A	V	A	R	K	A
I	H	A	K	M	J	A	I	D	L	N	B	A	E	R
N	Y	M	O	E	M	H	N	O	H	B	C	H	I	D
O	D	S	H	D	I	I	N	A	H	S	Y	C	T	S
K	N	E	I	Y	V	E	C	T	U	N	I	M	H	O
P	A	Y	G	L	A	K	E	R	M	A	C	K	I	S
L	R	H	A	C	N	I	G	O	W	D	E	T	O	C

RANDY HUNDLEY
FERNANDO RAMSEY
CLYDE MCCULLOUGH
BULL (BRUCE) EDWARDS
ALVIN DARK
STAN HACK
JORGE PEDRE
BILL BONHAM

Regular Righthanders

N	A	P	I	D	E	R	E	Z	N	I	P	A	U	E
R	O	N	A	L	A	D	J	A	K	E	R	S	O	N
R	I	S	P	W	U	V	L	I	T	I	N	E	L	O
J	O	S	R	C	I	N	E	E	M	I	E	N	D	T
O	D	B	E	E	A	L	B	W	K	T	A	M	I	S
N	S	A	E	C	T	R	D	L	E	M	O	M	O	E
L	Z	E	S	R	O	T	I	I	F	N	S	D	T	V
I	E	B	N	B	T	W	A	F	F	T	G	B	D	E
E	O	E	E	O	N	O	O	P	O	R	N	E	I	T
B	Y	R	R	A	J	C	R	D	E	P	E	A	R	S
E	G	D	E	N	N	G	D	I	S	I	L	N	N	T
R	S	D	I	I	T	A	U	N	V	X	G	A	A	R
C	H	A	V	E	R	U	L	O	B	E	T	G	V	U
I	E	E	M	D	A	R	V	I	D	S	R	J	E	K
S	K	U	R	T	M	I	L	L	E	R	A	A	O	R

BOB SCANLAN
DEAN WILKINS
ROBERTO RIVERA
PETE BROBERG
STEVE STONE
REGGIE PATTERSON
JON LIEBER
KEVIN COFFMAN
KURT MILLER
DOUG JONES
JIM TODD
TIM STODDARD
DAVE WENGERT

39

N A H A L L A C S E M A J O S
K O M A S A I J E M M A S T H
E E T E E O K C A M E V E T S
N S N N R U D N O B A V O N O
N N C H R O H A R O E T E V S
E E I D E O M A F O G H E I U
T H E T D N H E N N E T V R H
O I T R R L D T Z O F A O A N
O B I I L A I E R I D E R T N
F R W O M V M P R E S M T O L
Y N E R E S H Y V S T D I N E
R A L R E N E E R L O L E T A
R D O X I O T E S R I N A T R
A S E N J S A L L T E H W W D
B I L L E V E R I T T J A K Y

LEE SMITH
TED SIZEMORE
JERRY MARTIN
BILL EVERITT
JAMES CALLAHAN
WALTER THORNTON
STEVE ONTIVEROS
STEVE DAVIS
KEN HENDERSON
SAM MEJIAS
TIM DONAHUE
STEVE MACKO
BARRY FOOTE

Simply Some Of My Favorites

B	C	E	F	F	I	L	C	T	U	S	K	C	I	R
O	K	A	R	L	J	T	O	N	S	K	I	C	E	B
M	A	E	L	P	E	A	P	S	G	M	H	R	A	D
A	D	T	N	Y	H	O	M	A	E	R	O	K	T	T
M	L	J	E	T	K	I	R	I	I	N	S	R	N	N
O	I	U	O	C	M	Y	L	S	E	C	E	E	E	E
Z	E	K	L	E	G	E	S	N	A	M	R	E	H	R
E	E	I	E	A	G	P	R	N	O	R	O	P	K	A
S	F	N	E	L	E	I	O	C	E	R	O	Y	R	P
A	O	T	U	I	U	S	R	I	K	A	T	L	E	K
J	T	D	E	N	A	M	P	A	R	E	N	O	Y	R
I	O	R	O	Y	E	N	J	O	R	A	R	V	N	A
S	H	I	D	F	A	S	T	G	I	D	S	R	N	M
E	V	I	R	U	P	S	O	I	B	U	I	E	O	D
T	U	R	J	O	H	N	S	J	I	M	M	E	T	S

KENT MERCKER
JUAN PIERRE
MARK PARENT
JOSE NUNEZ
JAMIE MOYER
HERMAN SEGELKE
PHIL NORTON
GARY GAETTI
CHRIS SPEIER
JOE GIRARDI
MIKE LUM
RICK SUTCLIFFE

41

T	R	U	A	G	I	E	R	F	D	R	A	W	O	H
U	P	E	M	A	X	F	L	A	C	K	U	T	L	E
N	N	N	A	M	S	E	L	E	H	T	D	O	A	N
N	R	A	N	D	Y	J	A	C	K	S	O	N	W	R
O	O	M	N	P	T	O	H	C	R	I	C	Y	R	Y
B	T	E	T	F	I	N	S	U	T	R	C	W	E	R
Y	T	E	T	A	O	L	R	E	C	V	A	O	N	O
R	O	R	A	S	R	I	A	I	I	N	S	M	Z	D
R	K	F	I	T	M	E	M	D	F	O	E	A	O	R
O	N	K	H	S	A	B	M	R	M	R	Y	C	N	I
J	A	C	K	O	N	E	I	L	L	E	I	K	I	G
O	B	U	C	A	J	R	J	Y	M	N	T	K	C	U
I	E	B	A	T	A	Y	C	A	L	O	D	U	B	E
B	O	F	J	E	N	K	I	N	S	L	E	P	O	Z
I	X	W	S	M	A	I	L	L	I	W	O	T	T	O

OTTO WILLIAMS
IRV NOREN
LES MANN
OTTO KNABE
HOWARD FREIGAU
HENRY RODRIGUEZ
F. (FERGIE) JENKINS
RANDY JACKSON
JIM MARSHALL
JON LIEBER
JACK O'NEILL
MAX FLACK
JACK HIATT
TONY WOMACK
BUCK FREEMAN

Through the Years

Z	A	H	J	I	M	L	A	N	D	O	H	J	O	F
T	O	T	S	E	V	E	T	D	R	T	I	R	R	E
I	B	I	C	H	A	N	K	E	O	M	E	I	G	T
W	L	F	F	I	E	O	N	T	T	T	T	D	N	A
L	A	F	G	R	A	L	L	O	N	Z	I	A	E	T
L	M	I	R	H	E	U	D	E	M	R	G	K	T	E
O	C	R	A	A	A	D	P	O	D	E	L	K	S	I
M	I	G	D	P	E	R	L	N	N	I	V	E	L	N
Z	R	Y	O	T	A	L	A	U	W	J	A	M	E	N
T	E	M	N	C	O	T	D	Y	D	R	O	P	S	E
I	R	M	B	W	S	M	R	E	M	E	V	N	I	B
R	E	O	I	E	I	R	U	A	R	A	R	S	E	A
F	B	T	T	J	A	S	P	E	G	F	C	U	R	S
S	Z	E	F	H	E	E	L	I	U	A	M	K	S	O
T	P	R	E	T	S	A	J	Y	N	N	N	O	L	B

FRITZ MOLLWITZ
SHELDON JONES
JIM DUNEGAN
PETE STANDRIDGE
TOMMY GRIFFITH
BOB CARPENTER
PAUL TOTH

FRED LUDERUS
JIM TODD
FRED LEAR
HARRY WILKE
RAY MACK
PAT RAGAN
BENNIE TATE

Did You Ever Catch These Guys Play?

```
R K I C O W R A L P I K I N R
E N B T Y T E X S O R R E M E
K A O E T H E M K A A M O J F
C T R S A D U J N N E B J O F
A Y C U N N Q D D R I J L H A
H E E K V E Y Y R L G L I N H
T L R O W B H I L E I H E C C
E I S G O U T P N R T F V H S
O A I B N T L E E A P U R U E
M B B D R U O V E T M I T R I
E D L A M L A H I A S A Z R M
N E N M I L L O A K V N S Y M
Y E E V R L C O R D E H H L I
W R E A I C E U K P U R O O J
T R E B N A G Y O M A C O N J
```

RANDY BOBB
JOHN STEPHENSON
BILL PLUMMER
JIMMIE SCHAFFER
ED BAILEY
RANDY HUNDLEY
BILL HEATH
GENE OLIVER
MERRITT RANEW
MOE THACKER
EARL AVERILL
JOHN CHURRY

They Stepped Up To the Plate

F	L	I	N	D	S	T	R	U	M	R	A	V	H	T
D	Y	G	A	F	U	N	O	D	I	L	E	C	T	P
R	N	E	H	O	L	Y	B	E	S	R	Y	A	I	E
A	A	J	W	O	F	I	T	P	E	M	O	T	M	N
L	N	U	N	L	S	Z	A	K	Y	C	U	T	S	A
L	A	K	N	A	O	N	L	A	C	E	O	N	E	M
I	C	Y	U	E	G	A	R	C	D	N	T	K	I	T
L	M	L	A	L	W	R	E	I	Y	A	P	I	L	L
E	M	O	E	Y	U	T	O	T	P	I	S	L	L	A
N	I	R	R	M	V	E	A	M	A	Z	E	B	I	E
E	J	R	Y	L	O	Y	A	D	Y	O	S	I	W	G
G	A	N	T	B	L	E	R	E	H	B	T	N	T	R
H	O	P	I	O	T	A	E	F	A	E	B	G	E	O
T	P	A	R	K	R	A	B	R	A	G	B	O	B	E
M	U	N	O	Y	A	R	R	U	M	D	E	R	B	G

BOB GARBARK
F. (FREDDIE) LINDSTROM
GENE LILLARD
TONY MURRAY
AL SPANGLER
TONY TAYLOR
BOBBY MORGAN
RED MURRAY
GEORGE ALTMAN
WILLIE SMITH
HARRY WALKER
JIM MCANANY

An Afternoon Game In the 1960s Saw These Guys

B	R	A	N	A	M	U	A	B	K	N	A	R	F	A
A	E	X	T	O	D	N	E	B	O	B	B	U	H	L
O	D	E	D	E	N	N	Y	T	C	H	I	P	S	E
H	N	O	S	L	E	I	R	B	A	G	N	E	L	L
S	A	I	L	T	O	U	D	R	I	R	V	S	A	L
M	W	R	G	F	B	U	R	O	E	N	A	E	N	E
O	N	K	V	S	O	Y	J	T	A	M	K	G	C	B
T	E	E	I	E	B	P	S	A	O	V	T	H	D	P
E	L	L	Y	R	Y	N	H	H	C	A	I	T	E	M
F	L	J	I	N	E	K	T	I	O	K	H	W	R	A
E	I	G	A	L	H	K	U	R	L	A	S	M	T	C
O	H	T	S	C	N	C	Y	E	A	L	P	O	O	N
T	H	O	D	A	B	B	I	L	N	R	I	C	N	O
H	R	I	R	R	F	I	Y	R	B	N	M	P	O	R
T	O	F	K	L	S	U	H	C	O	W	E	R	S	T

RON CAMPBELL
ADOLFO PHILLIPS
HARVEY KUENN
FRANK BAUMANN
ELLIS BURTON
BOB BUHL

HARRY BRIGHT
RICH NYE
LEN GABRIELSON
FRANK THOMAS
LOU JACKSON

They Called the Outfield Their Office

```
H K I K I C U Y L E R A N D N
G C T E H U P A E E R S O N I
H A H N G A F L U S T T A H J
E C B A A Y I E B E R M A C O
B F A L R N O R C E I C D B D
N O I E Y L E I K R K M A T E
H O B N L S I S R W C B N E R
A T N A I Y A E I N E A E V I
N E O A D P M L G H K O L S N
K R K L E D S M E I W U A H S
S L N D Y O I R O L L E M T A
A B O O N C M S I T D B T N M
U D L E G A R I T O P I E E E
E L A G N I K K C I H C U R P
R O C E R G L E D Y B B O B T
```

PETE WHISENANT
LLOYD MERRIMAN
BOBBY DEL GRECO
CHARLIE GILBERT
KIKI CUYLER
TOMMY LEACH
CHICK KING
BOB ADDIS
HANK SAUER
BABE HERMAN
HACK WILSON
AL KAISER

More Names On the Roster

L	I	S	H	A	L	R	E	I	L	L	Y	T	S	H
S	P	E	S	E	R	A	L	P	F	O	O	T	L	C
A	T	E	M	A	Y	K	C	I	R	N	I	C	F	I
R	H	E	T	O	J	U	N	R	Y	O	A	R	A	V
W	E	S	V	E	L	O	E	K	V	R	O	S	E	O
C	D	L	G	E	T	H	A	U	T	H	H	C	J	M
L	M	I	T	N	T	U	N	E	T	O	E	A	M	U
A	O	J	L	U	F	R	R	R	O	T	K	R	N	D
Y	R	I	L	M	B	E	A	G	E	I	Y	M	A	K
B	R	M	A	S	L	Y	A	C	E	D	D	E	P	C
R	I	N	Y	L	Y	I	N	M	H	O	L	R	R	I
Y	S	O	I	N	R	H	A	N	S	S	N	Y	B	N
A	J	O	H	N	R	Y	L	I	H	O	E	R	N	T
N	T	L	L	A	P	N	N	O	D	O	N	L	E	N
T	O	M	S	I	R	R	O	M	D	E	J	O	N	S

HAL REILLY
CARTER ELLIOTT
PETE TURGEON
LUTHER ROY
JAKIE MAY
DONN PALL
RED LYNN
TONY KAUFMANN
ED MORRIS
NICK DUMOVICH
JOHNNY BUTLER
CLAY BRYANT
STEVE TRACHSEL

Who's On Deck?

G	R	E	B	I	R	F	E	I	N	R	E	B	S	W
T	L	W	H	N	T	F	S	T	U	B	E	T	O	N
I	W	U	O	M	A	E	K	I	D	R	E	H	L	A
J	O	M	A	X	T	H	L	Q	O	V	C	O	E	L
D	P	P	U	R	U	I	N	M	E	A	R	W	G	U
A	O	T	I	O	C	E	E	D	F	U	S	A	H	L
N	R	H	S	O	D	Z	I	T	I	W	R	R	H	P
N	M	A	R	O	I	L	X	E	N	E	L	D	A	E
Y	E	L	I	S	L	O	P	A	J	Y	U	J	R	D
T	O	E	D	A	A	O	T	A	T	K	C	O	B	V
A	N	E	R	K	L	N	S	C	L	L	I	H	E	I
Y	T	D	L	I	M	E	W	B	I	P	L	N	S	T
L	L	E	H	C	T	I	M	E	K	I	M	S	A	N
O	B	A	M	D	Y	V	R	A	M	S	G	O	G	E
R	T	N	O	L	A	N	M	A	R	T	I	N	E	S

STEVE DILLARD

HOWARD JOHNSON

TED SIZEMORE

MIKE MITCHELL

BERNIE FRIBERG

DANNY TAYLOR

Late 1940s Fellas

F	W	I	D	E	X	M	D	A	B	G	H	M	E	N
C	N	X	J	U	C	E	Y	Z	T	R	O	I	V	Z
H	I	O	R	L	T	O	P	H	I	N	T	S	U	N
S	L	N	S	E	A	C	C	E	K	F	R	O	H	E
I	N	H	R	R	K	I	H	D	C	E	J	A	T	H
D	N	E	B	E	E	C	U	L	B	L	L	D	I	C
K	O	I	O	R	B	B	A	M	E	J	U	E	K	S
O	M	Y	M	D	I	O	A	H	E	O	T	G	D	K
R	E	R	L	E	P	H	D	F	N	E	N	M	O	N
D	E	N	L	E	C	M	F	S	F	E	D	A	C	A
H	B	G	A	F	L	C	E	I	S	I	R	S	R	H
U	P	R	F	K	O	A	I	T	J	E	L	R	L	D
R	O	I	V	A	F	T	D	S	O	W	J	C	A	B
S	L	G	T	I	Z	A	R	E	E	F	O	A	I	W
C	L	A	R	E	N	C	E	M	A	D	D	E	R	N

HANK SCHENZ
WARREN HACKER
HAL JEFFCOAT
CLARENCE MADDERN
JESS DOBERNIC
CLIFF ABERSON
MONK DUBIEL
DUTCH LEONARD
HERM REICH
DOYLE LADE
CLIFF CHAMBERS

Strictly Southpaws

T	D	O	W	O	L	B	A	O	T	N	O	D	E	N
J	H	A	I	S	E	N	O	J	Y	C	R	E	P	O
D	I	V	N	E	H	C	O	R	A	L	E	V	A	D
H	A	M	E	N	R	E	A	L	L	I	T	V	T	B
S	N	O	B	U	Y	E	T	E	Y	E	W	U	A	I
O	N	S	W	R	O	F	D	O	L	A	O	R	I	S
P	R	A	W	L	I	D	R	L	I	H	T	I	N	A
S	O	N	Y	M	A	L	O	I	C	N	K	C	I	T
T	G	F	I	W	I	P	L	A	E	B	N	H	T	A
O	X	I	E	K	E	N	E	H	A	N	M	N	E	Y
A	L	B	T	I	C	T	F	N	E	O	D	Y	E	D
B	U	T	W	A	D	I	C	K	O	A	N	E	A	D
R	A	O	Q	U	I	N	T	O	N	E	R	Y	O	U
M	H	I	B	R	E	T	A	N	I	H	I	T	L	B
Z	E	D	N	A	N	R	E	H	E	I	L	L	I	W

ART NEHF
BUD TEACHOUT
RUBE WADDELL
WILLIE HERNANDEZ
MATT KILROY

PERCY JONES
JIM BRILLHEART
HOWIE POLLET
DANNY FRIEND
DAVE LAROCHE

Durocher's Dudes

```
A R T J O S E M A J O E L C E
T N O C O L K B I K O M I S S
I Q O G P E G C O H U T P U T
H J U S E O P T A R L H C T E
M O A E I R O E E D I A P F V
L U Y M Z L M L P L A J A A E
R L N T L E L E G I B C R E B
B O A E W I U A T J T U M W A
W O S H M I G G C Z G O R E R
H A O B E L L M I Y G V N D B
O X O T I I A H R R N E V E E
G B I A S R M R E N D N R E R
R W N A T D A M E L X O H A Y
I O C I Y L A M I Z M R R O D
F U N N E D A Y S J A C R R J
```

STEVE BARBER
LARRY GURA
JOHNNY CALLISON
CLEO JAMES
JIMMIE HALL
ROGER METZGER
R. (ROBERTO) RODRIGUEZ
BOOTS DAY
BOB MILLER
HOYT WILHELM
J. C. MARTIN
PHIL GAGLIANO
JOE PEPITONE

My Kingdom For a Closer

```
H P C L Y D E S H O U N D O T
A M A X L C G O Y E R I N R L
R L D U R E L U N C C B A C I
R L I T L A S R O K T C I T T
Y M O N U D I S M A B O D V T
P L A I D N E A U O T R A Z E
E O N R I Y N R B R A H T E N
R P A U K V M H R H K R K D I
K I R T I F E C Z I A C O O T
O S O L F N R U D M N I A R N
W A L Y D F B E Y A H G E J E
S E O L S N L D E C N U E F L
K R E I H C N A O M O I A R A
I Y N O T A O Y G C A N E R V
M O J E R N O R T S O N R L V
```

LINDY MCDANIEL
HARRY PERKOWSKI
BOB HENDLEY
JOHN BUZHARDT
PAUL DERRINGER
V. (VITO) VALENTINETTI
RANDY MARTZ
JACK RUSSELL
DICK MANVILLE
CLYDE SHOUN
MARK FREEMAN

Could Be Your Right Hand Man

```
N A M R A G E K I M D E N I B
O D A L L E N U I E V E R D M
U L Y L A N E D L I M H N A H
R O R R F Y R C A I A A N O I
I N E A R O L D K K L N R M V
C R I Z B E N E E E Y R A A A
H A T H I N P S U S A R N M N
G E C P I E Y T E V K C S O C
A I G O R O S O A C E K O R E
R M L E S E A N L P A N D K P
C A Z K G N E A A O H I E R A
E J I R E M R G I B O L C E G
S N O M I K E G A R M A L B E
O E D A N B Y Y R R E P T A P
G V J T I M W O R R E L L O A
```

MIKE PEREZ
TIM WORRELL
MARK CLARK
MIKE GARMAN
GEORGE STUELAND
A. (ANTONIO) ALFONSECA
JAMIE ARNOLD
RICH GARCES
RICH BORDI
VANCE PAGE
JAIME NAVARRO
MANNY SEOANE

Who's On First?

J	A	Y	L	L	E	K	E	G	R	O	E	G	P	I
I	E	H	M	M	I	R	G	E	I	L	R	A	H	C
M	E	S	T	H	A	V	E	L	E	W	U	S	O	S
M	H	A	R	Y	C	R	O	B	I	L	N	U	R	N
I	C	A	S	O	T	I	N	D	C	O	V	O	W	I
E	U	R	J	B	N	R	E	A	T	E	N	I	P	L
F	B	T	I	I	A	N	V	R	U	T	L	O	I	L
O	D	W	P	P	M	A	O	Q	M	L	I	R	W	O
X	E	A	I	E	R	H	R	C	I	R	E	N	D	C
X	A	L	L	E	T	U	I	E	K	I	E	O	G	R
E	C	L	T	E	O	E	S	C	A	C	T	H	I	E
M	A	T	R	B	L	M	W	S	K	U	U	O	E	P
I	A	D	T	R	I	O	C	A	E	M	H	H	D	P
N	N	A	F	T	I	I	N	T	R	L	A	I	C	I
A	P	D	H	D	V	M	S	G	E	D	L	N	O	R

RIP RUSSELL
CHUCK CONNORS
ED BOUCHEE
DICK WARD
WILLIE SMITH
RIPPER COLLINS
ANDRE THORNTON
HERM REICH
DALE LONG
PAT BOURQUE
VIC SAIER
GEORGE KELLY
JIMMIE FOXX
CHARLIE GRIMM

Pitching Staff of 2001

```
S C W E A L I E W B O B D U C
W E B F R A G I V R O A X O Y
J N K H R E L O E L V P N J J
J O O S U L B S D I N A B U I
F O U S O Y S N D R R D A A M
I W E H S A A W O B O N E N C
Z A M B F A E Y M S T O E C N
W A K F O A I A N A A P N R O
N M F U T R Z H V U O J T U D
P E T H O S O A C E T L I Z R
J S E T O S R W R T I O L C O
T R O L I E N B S O T A M A G
S N R O Z G A I V K C O E D M
B A K E R G S A T A I S C G O
C L A E I R H Y F E K I M S T
```

JASON BERE
SCOTT CHIASSON
DAVID WEATHERS
CARLOS ZAMBRANO
TOM GORDON
JOE BOROWSKI
JUAN CRUZ
JEFF FASSERO
MIKE FYHRIE
WILL OHMAN

More Nicknames

Y	T	A	E	R	E	N	M	A	H	Z	U	R	B	F
M	N	W	A	S	O	T	A	V	E	Y	E	B	R	O
Y	A	O	I	A	E	A	W	T	U	L	D	O	C	I
B	Y	D	S	T	X	D	U	M	A	R	C	E	W	P
U	Q	A	M	L	C	G	A	H	C	K	C	O	S	A
R	U	I	L	O	O	H	C	L	S	F	U	M	E	U
T	I	N	B	P	N	H	R	M	Y	D	O	T	D	L
E	N	E	K	N	V	K	C	I	N	K	E	I	E	L
Y	T	Y	A	I	E	I	M	I	C	P	R	K	R	O
E	E	L	T	N	N	D	T	E	N	K	I	O	E	B
S	R	K	I	T	J	E	I	H	Y	H	E	R	P	E
D	S	N	I	W	A	H	A	C	S	E	S	R	H	G
R	I	R	T	R	O	O	D	E	A	R	R	I	T	U
I	E	R	H	I	N	D	O	W	I	N	S	O	W	E
B	R	U	S	E	T	R	E	M	W	O	D	N	A	S

PORKY (DOYLE) LADE
BRUZ (RALPH) HAMNER
MAD MONK (RUSS) MEYER
TWITCH (MARV) RICKERT
SWISH (BILL) NICHOLSON
ROCKS (HARRY) MCINTIRE
BIRDS EYE (HARRY) TRUBY
SANDOW (SAM) MERTES

A Little Chatter In the Infield

N	O	S	R	E	K	L	I	W	S	I	T	R	U	C
M	Z	F	R	A	N	C	I	S	F	L	A	N	T	G
A	L	E	I	W	T	Y	B	I	E	R	S	D	A	L
N	T	D	U	S	U	Y	O	N	A	H	R	N	O	I
N	E	R	C	Q	C	F	N	F	K	A	T	A	D	V
Y	N	V	E	A	R	H	C	E	H	A	V	E	R	E
A	O	U	E	K	R	A	A	O	S	E	Y	O	A	R
L	R	P	D	T	C	R	M	D	A	W	C	I	S	T
E	M	E	I	N	R	E	P	O	M	G	L	U	P	N
X	G	T	C	P	O	D	B	N	L	E	E	T	W	O
A	I	E	E	M	K	R	E	N	E	A	Y	C	I	M
N	G	R	T	A	C	T	L	E	N	I	Z	E	N	L
D	O	K	E	K	S	P	L	H	L	E	M	N	R	A
E	N	O	S	U	H	F	F	E	J	P	L	I	O	S
R	E	V	A	S	O	P	U	T	S	M	E	G	N	G

JEFF HUSON
MANNY ALEXANDER
CURTIS WILKERSON
NORM GIGON
GONZALO MARQUEZ
CHAD MEYERS
LEE ELIA
GLENN BECKERT
RON DUNN

Love Those Latinos

Z	E	N	I	T	R	A	M	O	L	E	M	R	A	C
I	H	C	R	S	U	S	E	J	E	D	N	A	V	I
L	E	A	N	O	L	A	O	I	M	U	R	E	C	Z
I	A	Z	O	I	B	S	E	I	S	M	E	A	A	E
R	U	N	A	R	E	E	K	L	E	D	R	N	M	L
R	A	K	E	O	E	E	R	L	E	L	I	A	M	A
U	N	B	R	D	P	U	M	T	O	P	N	I	L	Z
L	A	T	N	E	R	A	G	S	O	N	K	A	I	N
E	I	O	R	N	R	A	L	I	Y	P	Y	F	M	O
Z	E	E	Z	T	Y	E	C	T	F	A	E	R	R	G
B	Z	A	I	A	Z	A	R	E	Y	S	A	N	O	L
R	D	N	T	C	R	I	Y	B	S	C	U	I	A	U
O	E	W	A	O	L	I	B	N	A	O	R	S	T	A
Z	N	N	H	L	P	O	A	T	I	R	J	T	E	R
E	O	M	O	R	B	A	T	U	R	C	I	E	Z	J

ROBERTO PENA
HORACIO PINA
JESUS FIGUEROA
CARLOS LEZCANO
RAUL GONZALEZ
CARMELO MARTINEZ
JOSE CARDENAL
IVAN DEJESUS
MANNY TRILLO
JOSE ORTIZ
MIKE PEREZ
BOBBY AYALA

In the Infield

```
F I N T E R O B E R S T A G D
L Y A T I A B T E C W I I O S
O V L F A D R U V O L N N E N
N K I L I B G L Y E E Y V A T
R O C C A H I E S O J A L R K
E A S I L N S L K M R L A K C
Y N Y K T A N K L G I W O M I
A E P G C T R O E M E T I E P
H C R C R A A O C T C U H R E
S I O G M I J M S E A C D L I
Y D P A S N M Y Y E I R A Y D
T O E T L R M E D B E Z R B D
R V N L O M E R S N B P T I E
A E O N I C I R B L A O S I T
M Y R J O H N N N Y A R B A F
```

EARL SMITH
RAY GRIMES
MARK KOENIG
RANDY JACKSON
VIC LAROSE
BILL MCCABE
EDDIE PICK
DOC CASEY
BOBBY MATTICK
NORM MCMILLAN
MARTY SHAY
JIMMY STEWART
JOE GRAVES

You Never Saw These Guys On TV

G	N	I	L	L	I	W	Z	H	C	T	U	D	A	Y
B	E	Z	I	V	O	C	U	D	T	A	P	R	E	C
R	I	S	E	F	I	X	U	G	Y	H	E	L	C	M
O	H	L	I	E	R	N	A	B	O	S	S	K	I	L
Y	A	L	L	C	R	O	C	U	N	M	Y	C	U	N
P	O	R	C	S	W	A	D	E	E	L	K	E	N	Y
A	A	Y	E	T	W	I	M	H	B	E	S	T	O	C
R	V	U	E	L	O	E	E	E	Y	A	N	G	I	N
M	O	O	L	L	L	I	E	D	D	I	R	A	F	I
E	N	T	A	C	L	I	O	N	E	K	A	T	O	W
L	U	C	M	L	A	O	M	D	E	M	N	U	O	F
E	I	E	O	G	L	R	H	D	O	Y	E	A	H	N
E	L	R	J	A	Y	O	T	D	R	I	R	Y	R	T
C	W	I	N	A	X	O	T	E	E	A	L	I	E	F
E	C	R	O	W	A	Y	D	U	R	O	W	H	O	R

PAUL CARTER
MICKEY DOOLAN
ROY PARMELEE
ROLLIE HEMSLEY
ED HOLLEY
BILL SWEENEY
C. (CHARLIE) WIEDEMEYER

CLEM CLEMENS
DUTCH ZWILLING
VINCE BARTON
FRANK DEMAREE
WARD MILLER

Great First Names, Eh?

R	A	N	T	L	E	B	O	D	I	C	S	O	S	Y
O	E	N	A	I	L	U	R	G	O	D	L	L	M	C
W	O	F	O	M	E	E	N	O	L	M	I	A	E	N
D	I	R	E	S	Z	T	D	I	A	G	N	D	O	L
Y	A	B	J	A	K	U	H	N	B	G	L	E	S	I
E	V	E	I	T	H	C	G	J	E	A	P	R	I	X
L	O	R	M	D	D	C	I	L	N	W	A	T	R	O
L	A	K	Y	I	I	U	S	D	E	I	K	E	J	N
I	W	O	P	L	S	A	R	Y	E	G	A	R	E	E
O	N	U	E	T	L	U	W	T	N	C	N	O	U	R
T	C	A	I	A	M	E	N	A	T	A	N	A	S	T
T	O	N	Z	A	C	Y	R	E	C	K	M	A	X	E
H	B	A	M	E	C	U	S	E	R	D	O	R	L	R
I	R	A	D	E	N	O	G	V	E	Y	E	D	E	I
T	E	S	H	T	I	M	S	Y	R	R	A	H	A	G

HARRY SMITH
GERMANY SCHAEFER
ANGEL SALAZAR
CED LANDRUM
ROWDY ELLIOTT
ANGEL GUZMAN
CUPID CHILDS
LANCE DICKSON
TURK WENDELL

They Wore the Uniform

R I P S S K N A B E I L L I W
E B O B D E R N I E R C Y P A
L O R A K E N O D E A N M E Z
L X E I K U C S O L B A Z S T
I O G S T P D R N N L E N L H
M R I D Y G P E S S H O J O A
C A L C U T E D I C M U O M N
O R L A I M L N N M R K B S K
D F I W A T N A I E S O H A G
C E W N L E S S N C V A V T R
R L R O D Y T T O A M L E J I
E R E T E R R T Y M G N E I F
N A T R U O T O N U F A I B F
O H W C K E L C T I H O E A I
S C N A R A I S C O G G E R N

DOC MILLER
CURT SIMMONS
W. (WAYNE) TERWILLIGER
DENNIS LAMP
SCOTT SANDERSON
CAL NEEMAN
HANK GRIFFIN
BOB DERNIER
REY SANCHEZ
WILLIE BANKS
HOOKS COTTER
KEN O'DEA

On the Mound

```
S N I L L O C L I H P B I S M
O L L A C C M H C T U D T I S
N D L U A P L L L B H A K T O
U B I L L Y H U P T E E I R P
H O A C R I A A I N C E T U A
T E R E K P T D J A M V H C N
E T H E H T I E M N C E C F U
S N O S E R I P A H I B R F O
O I O R E D B D N C A A U I H
J J S M D E P R R S O C H L S
A O N I L K U E V O K H C C E
N O J L S U C C I U W E N Y D
R E T I R W E I D C A R E R Y
O L L E S S U F D E R F L A L
Y E N W A H S I E K M R O H C
```

DICK TIDROW
CLYDE SHOUN
FRED FUSSELL
MIKE CAMPBELL
LEN CHURCH
CLIFF CURTIS
RON MERIDITH
PHIL COLLINS
DICK DROTT
JOSH PAUL
DUTCH MCCALL

They Even Sound Like Ballplayers

J	O	R	G	C	E	S	J	A	N	E	R	U	S	K
A	I	R	E	O	A	O	G	N	I	O	M	J	E	R
L	E	G	X	G	H	L	T	I	W	C	A	N	Z	A
R	E	O	G	N	N	S	K	D	D	B	T	N	A	I
R	S	F	K	E	I	I	Y	O	O	B	O	O	C	G
B	E	A	T	E	R	E	R	B	O	O	D	L	K	S
O	N	P	H	Y	L	S	L	T	G	N	H	N	T	P
E	I	L	P	L	Y	O	T	A	S	Z	C	E	A	E
F	A	J	I	I	C	E	M	A	I	U	V	E	Y	N
F	A	O	I	K	N	Y	R	P	T	E	O	K	L	T
I	T	T	E	F	S	L	Z	K	R	Z	A	L	O	E
T	R	R	I	P	M	A	A	A	U	L	I	A	R	R
O	T	E	O	E	B	K	I	H	C	N	Y	L	D	E
N	L	T	B	E	E	N	T	F	Y	A	D	R	I	L
D	E	R	L	N	I	T	R	A	M	D	E	E	P	S

KENT BOTTENFIELD
CURTIS GOODWIN
LOU STRINGER
CAL KOONCE
JOHN KANE
ZACK TAYLOR
STEVE RAIN
ZIP ZABEL
BOB LOCKER
ED LYNCH
AL HEIST

Short Timers

Y	B	O	T	D	E	Z	A	D	N	U	R	L	A	W
J	I	G	C	O	L	F	A	N	D	U	E	K	I	J
L	O	F	E	G	U	W	I	U	K	O	T	A	J	O
L	E	H	I	O	K	S	T	T	A	C	S	V	O	H
E	N	T	N	O	F	C	A	R	E	M	A	E	H	N
H	A	E	E	N	H	F	T	K	A	I	D	A	N	J
C	R	U	D	K	Y	W	Z	D	E	I	N	T	S	O
T	O	P	N	I	I	R	A	A	B	R	U	O	U	H
I	Y	A	E	L	R	L	Y	O	H	E	R	N	L	N
M	B	B	S	E	E	R	D	A	D	N	T	T	L	J
E	L	O	D	B	O	A	O	U	N	K	I	R	I	O
K	N	I	E	T	O	N	O	C	S	I	R	E	V	H
I	C	R	L	I	E	L	Y	O	D	Y	R	R	A	L
M	B	O	B	H	U	M	P	H	R	E	Y	S	N	A
F	F	U	D	L	I	K	E	T	E	P	R	O	N	N

MIKE MITCHELL
RED CORRIDEN
REBEL ADAMS
ART WILSON
JOHN SULLIVAN
GEOFF ZAHN
BOB HUMPHREYS
DUTCH KNABE
LARRY DOYLE
PETE KILDUFF
JOHNNY RYAN

66

W	C	D	A	V	E	H	I	L	L	M	A	N	D	A
T	H	O	M	M	O	T	L	A	H	G	F	G	Y	S
R	S	E	V	E	E	H	C	L	I	G	R	I	V	L
E	E	E	I	O	A	U	L	S	H	A	E	R	C	R
K	E	T	L	H	T	V	R	A	N	O	D	A	R	O
S	N	F	L	L	O	C	O	B	M	C	M	C	E	W
A	U	I	L	O	I	O	H	A	M	L	E	H	Z	D
P	I	R	S	O	W	S	G	A	G	D	R	R	N	Y
E	S	E	T	O	W	Y	B	A	N	T	K	I	E	E
D	O	B	A	H	E	Y	R	U	Y	H	L	S	D	L
O	E	S	A	M	S	N	R	R	R	D	E	R	R	L
D	A	T	H	E	S	A	M	R	A	T	B	O	E	I
O	K	D	R	W	U	N	E	C	A	H	O	V	G	O
E	I	R	T	E	J	L	A	M	I	H	F	N	O	T
B	R	E	T	E	P	A	S	A	N	O	N	E	R	T

DODE PASKERT
ROGER DENZER
FRED MERKLE
VIRGIL CHEEVES
ROWDY ELLIOTT
HARRY WOLFE
HARRY WOLTER
DAVE HILLMAN
ELLIS BURTON

What Years Did We See These Guys?

J	E	R	O	M	E	W	I	L	L	I	A	M	S	N
O	G	K	B	I	L	T	H	O	J	M	O	G	I	I
H	I	N	D	O	Y	E	W	E	I	B	G	I	N	E
N	E	B	U	D	E	C	R	K	B	N	F	O	J	T
T	H	I	K	O	D	R	E	A	U	I	S	W	U	S
E	T	R	O	N	Y	G	T	O	M	L	L	A	E	N
Y	O	S	A	W	O	Y	Y	E	I	B	A	I	S	E
O	U	X	H	R	R	Y	N	W	A	D	N	L	T	T
R	V	I	D	R	N	I	E	O	R	S	D	T	I	R
S	T	O	E	O	E	U	N	A	H	V	E	O	C	A
E	N	J	H	U	Q	P	A	T	R	T	R	M	K	H
U	L	T	L	I	J	N	I	J	O	G	N	B	I	C
T	N	G	R	E	B	N	E	E	R	G	M	A	D	A
A	A	N	T	O	O	P	I	V	I	L	Y	U	E	S
L	E	H	C	S	U	E	R	L	U	A	P	T	N	W

ADAM GREENBERG
ANTHONY YOUNG
JEROME WILLIAMS
PAUL REUSCHEL
C. (CHUCK) HARTENSTEIN
JERRY WHITE
ENRIQUE WILSON
JERRY TABB
MIKE GORDON

More Boys of Summer

J	L	E	N	O	R	Y	T	E	N	Y	A	W	V	I
J	P	L	S	F	T	S	S	E	M	C	K	O	S	Y
L	I	S	E	T	Y	S	A	I	R	A	X	E	L	A
L	H	M	I	S	E	U	G	H	M	B	R	E	N	D
E	R	I	M	V	N	V	R	N	A	B	S	Y	O	R
D	O	S	H	Y	A	T	E	A	R	I	B	G	S	E
N	F	E	C	T	S	D	D	Y	N	O	E	U	A	V
E	I	S	O	O	O	H	N	K	E	N	N	I	E	A
W	H	R	E	N	T	S	E	O	K	R	E	M	L	E
K	T	T	B	A	P	T	R	C	R	C	K	E	A	W
R	M	A	N	G	E	W	P	T	K	H	I	E	M	E
U	A	S	M	P	E	O	E	E	S	A	P	R	S	I
T	S	E	L	R	I	P	K	L	R	I	R	O	I	L
S	E	Y	A	H	L	L	I	B	T	R	C	D	H	R
P	U	S	G	I	R	L	M	E	O	J	Y	E	T	O

RON DAVIS
MIKE PRENDERGAST
JIMMY SHECKARD
ELMER KOESTNER
ORLIE WEAVER
SCOTT PERRY
TURK WENDELL
WAYNE TYRONE
BILL HAYES
ALEX ARIAS
PETE KNISELY
MAL EASON
STEVE YERKES

The Armory

J	U	G	G	E	R	A	R	D	R	A	W	E	X	T
O	S	J	E	G	P	E	L	P	I	K	O	N	A	N
E	I	I	M	O	R	P	O	I	H	P	S	T	A	Y
K	A	M	K	K	R	E	A	D	B	T	O	M	I	R
R	Z	X	R	C	C	G	B	T	W	E	R	D	L	N
A	N	V	G	O	O	E	E	D	L	O	A	K	E	A
E	E	A	A	S	U	R	B	F	N	E	B	U	R	V
M	W	U	G	T	V	E	D	D	R	U	C	R	S	N
E	I	T	O	R	I	J	E	U	O	A	S	P	T	E
R	B	O	C	A	O	R	T	G	M	R	Z	M	O	B
D	O	N	Y	H	F	M	Q	A	P	L	L	I	I	F
C	A	T	S	F	N	O	E	U	X	F	I	E	E	J
R	E	L	I	F	M	O	T	K	E	I	L	H	O	R
K	C	A	J	E	S	S	I	S	I	S	M	E	P	J
E	S	T	O	J	H	E	N	I	D	M	O	L	R	T

JEFF HARTSOCK
ROD BECK
MIKE MORGAN
JIM SUNDBERG
PHIL MUDROCK
GEORGE FRAZIER

JUG GERARD
BEN VAN RYN
JOE KRAEMER
TOM FILER
FRED NORMAN
EL TAPPE

Cracker "Jacks"

```
J J J A C K I N F U A J O J T
T A I A C O L D K C A J A G H
A C C H C A R Y M C N C G L I
H K U K L K R O K I K O H E E
O W N K H I W H L L A R I J E
S A D A I A A A I E J E C A M
K R E J S Y R T L A M R O C O
C N O C D T T D C L A E N K H
A E N E E R J K Y W A H U A K
J R N L E B A M A L K C A J C
S N O L B K C S O N Y C E A A
S D L R E T S E I F P K C A J
D J A R R E P R A H K C A J S
E O T C E A T N O D S I O N A
R E J A C K H A M S T E L O R
```

JACK HARDY
JACK HARPER
JACK LAMABE
JACK WALLACE
JACK WARNER
JACK HAYDEN
JACK PFIESTER
JACK LITTRELL
JACK AKER

Did These Guys See Ivy In Their Dreams?

```
L G S B B O D N H O J I B E F
M E E Z A C A R T J A H N O R
D I E O F A N B Y H E J R T A
G O K M R T U D F R E D N A N
N O B E A G I O H A N W O K K
I T R A L G E A I A D R S E B
E B C U T Y E M S U V O D B A
L A B K A L N E A N R L I S U
K A T E E M L C H I O T V O M
K W I T W L N W H O S R A K H
C H E R A L I E Y U S E D I O
U N I D O I R R M I K E L M L
H A N G H E R A L R D E L O T
C O T T O J A L E D A N I T Z
D R A M I C T C H I N C B S A
```

FRANK BAUMHOLTZ	CHUCK KLEIN
JOHN DOBBS	LEE MAGEE
GEORGE MAISEL	EARL WEBB
BILL DAVIDSON	ART JAHN
CARMEN MAURO	MIKE LYNCH

Not Just Any Ol' Joe

E	D	A	C	E	O	J	O	A	Y	O	B	I	N	J
J	O	E	M	U	N	S	O	N	O	E	J	O	O	O
K	O	E	B	N	J	Y	J	E	J	O	S	E	D	E
J	J	I	E	J	N	O	F	O	M	N	J	Z	R	K
O	O	O	U	F	E	A	E	O	E	A	T	O	E	L
E	E	E	E	B	E	S	M	H	E	L	R	E	R	A
P	J	T	E	V	T	N	P	G	U	E	O	T	O	S
A	A	R	U	A	E	E	E	H	U	G	E	J	Y	S
D	R	A	N	N	T	R	C	M	O	L	H	J	A	M
Y	E	L	T	S	A	S	N	D	E	L	K	E	T	A
T	E	O	E	V	E	S	T	O	N	O	E	E	S	C
Y	K	O	T	O	M	O	I	T	N	U	J	E	O	K
H	J	O	J	E	O	J	I	T	R	A	D	E	O	J
S	R	A	G	N	I	N	R	E	D	E	O	J	R	J
C	H	D	O	Y	A	N	B	J	E	R	R	A	L	S

JOE MUNSON
JOE JAEGER
JOE BERRY
JOE STANLEY
JOE STEPHENSON
JOE KLUGMANN
JOE SCHULTZ
JOE VERNON
JOE HUGHES
JOE MARTY

Unusual Names, Don't You Think?

```
T N I K O P E I J O E H R I E
R O I T I N A V E N E O K V T
G E W T J D U E R D L P A R R
J M G A R L D O M Y X R I E E
P I A N H A B U A B G A G T B
H H G W E S M T R R L D U T L
Y E O G O T K D A B G O M O A
M N U Y E N T H E L I T L C A
M R N I I R S I S E E N S S W
O I T H C E S S P A P K T K E
T S C C L T J T R Y E S E O T
B I E B O F R D A E K B N O M
U P B O K U L F U T V N I H C
M U F U C V I C T O Z A I R O
B E K A L B F F I R E H S P T
```

FOOTSIE BLAIR
PINKY PITTENGER
JIGGER STATZ
TINY OSBORNE
BUBBLES HARGRAVE
SHERIFF BLAKE
CHINK TAYLOR
HOOKS COTTER
SPEED MARTIN
KID DURBIN

74

H	A	N	I	K	G	T	A	H	E	S	S	D	R	E
T	A	O	S	B	I	T	E	M	C	I	Y	C	U	T
E	I	R	D	E	O	T	I	F	R	O	H	S	O	A
B	Y	R	R	C	N	L	R	U	N	A	E	M	D	J
N	I	N	F	Y	V	O	T	E	R	G	M	R	I	A
N	A	E	S	E	S	Z	N	L	S	Y	O	M	K	M
Y	I	D	R	E	I	T	I	I	S	T	M	M	E	M
U	Y	B	A	R	H	E	E	H	U	Y	N	D	N	I
A	A	L	A	G	P	L	I	I	C	Q	S	S	T	E
N	X	S	A	I	A	E	R	O	N	T	S	B	H	S
C	E	F	C	D	L	M	O	A	R	F	D	I	H	P
C	E	K	O	D	M	N	E	A	Y	G	E	I	U	K
E	L	O	S	U	E	O	N	V	M	R	U	L	Y	L
N	A	R	E	Y	S	O	T	I	A	H	U	O	D	L
U	M	I	D	Y	E	N	A	H	D	D	O	T	L	T

CHARLIE PICK
EMIL VERBAN
JIMMY COONEY
HARRY STEINFELDT
TODD HANEY
TOM DALY
LUIS QUINONES
DAVE MAGADAN
TOMMY SHIELDS
CESAR IZTURIS

They Had a Share in '83

C	U	E	F	Y	A	N	O	T	U	N	E	T	E	P
S	R	M	I	C	T	M	F	I	V	Y	R	E	V	E
A	W	A	Y	N	E	N	O	R	D	H	A	G	E	N
V	B	E	I	L	S	Z	A	I	D	E	K	I	M	P
E	D	I	H	G	D	T	U	R	E	D	P	W	A	S
K	O	A	L	I	L	R	E	O	G	H	K	U	K	H
A	L	P	I	L	B	E	J	V	X	M	L	E	M	A
L	L	A	N	E	J	O	F	C	E	M	O	B	I	G
E	I	G	W	L	A	O	B	F	O	T	Z	T	J	U
V	C	R	E	M	I	E	H	S	E	G	R	A	H	A
E	Y	E	C	N	O	R	K	N	C	R	M	O	A	T
T	Y	S	O	H	T	A	B	S	S	H	T	E	U	E
S	A	X	K	A	U	O	J	O	G	O	U	S	M	T
F	E	I	T	R	O	U	F	E	L	R	N	L	H	O
D	N	A	L	E	R	O	M	H	T	I	E	K	Z	W

MIKE DIAZ
A. (ALAN) HARGESHEIMER
CRAIG LEFFERTS
RON CEY
TOM GRANT
WAYNE NORDHAGEN
STEVE LAKE
PAUL MOSKAU
BILL JOHNSON
MEL HALL
KEITH MORELAND
STEVE TROUT

L'il Nifties From the Fifties

L	L	O	R	E	E	M	R	E	D	N	A	V	J	T
W	W	A	T	O	B	L	A	T	E	L	A	D	W	O
T	A	C	A	R	L	S	A	W	A	T	S	K	I	P
S	R	L	Y	S	U	R	V	I	N	G	A	L	L	T
D	R	E	K	E	B	I	T	S	C	R	O	I	L	N
R	G	E	N	E	H	E	R	M	A	N	S	K	I	I
A	H	E	G	I	R	A	E	T	Z	O	E	N	E	O
H	O	M	N	L	K	C	T	I	N	O	F	O	R	D
C	T	J	O	E	O	H	O	O	V	R	A	T	A	A
I	S	L	E	L	B	B	P	O	L	K	I	S	M	H
R	O	R	E	S	O	A	M	L	P	I	J	N	S	S
D	F	H	C	A	K	A	K	I	A	E	V	E	D	G
E	T	M	Y	R	O	N	D	E	J	R	R	R	E	I
R	B	U	B	B	A	C	H	U	R	C	H	I	L	H
F	N	O	D	I	C	K	M	A	N	V	I	L	L	E

BUBBA CHURCH
GENE HERMANSKI
JIM BOLGER
RALPH KINER
CARL SAWATSKI
WILLIE RAMSDELL
J. (JOHNNY) VANDER MEER
GENE BAKER
DALE TALBOT
WALKER COOPER
DICK MANVILLE
FRED RICHARDS

Don't Forget These Names

```
N A R U N O B E K E Z T I U C
N L E E R G I J E O T F A R O
I A L O N U P L C A E R E U D
U O L A C I O D L U O L E V D
Q B W A H C A P H E T G I U H
Y E U E G S Y E S S R A T N G
P X B N S E R K R O G C A A J
M O I G T Y I A E B H F B R O
I K N I K D W G M R S E Y U H
W E H M M T K K U C G A T P N
A W O O I E L E N A O U E O R
Y A R B E D T O B A R D C M U
S E B R R H C L E P H I S O E
V A G L E W E D U K O J N L T
R E T R A R U D N O B E K E Z
```

ZEKE BONURA

RABBIT WARSTLER

WIMPY QUINN

DUTCH RUETHER

AUGIE GALAN

ROE SKIDMORE

DOC MARSHALL

KING COLE

GREEK GEORGE

WHITEY PLATT

HANK WYSE

GABE GABLER

More Pitchers From the Past

S	R	I	N	E	L	Y	T	Y	T	F	E	L	A	W
D	I	C	K	L	I	T	T	L	E	F	I	E	L	D
M	R	T	O	M	J	Y	W	A	L	Y	L	K	S	A
H	O	I	J	E	L	I	R	P	T	E	L	I	O	M
T	Y	R	D	R	E	Y	U	N	F	B	S	M	A	I
I	W	G	R	S	A	N	N	T	E	N	F	H	K	T
M	A	O	I	I	O	Y	Y	N	I	H	N	Z	O	B
S	L	F	V	N	E	T	N	K	N	O	L	I	V	A
E	K	O	A	G	Y	M	P	E	B	E	U	L	N	P
I	E	S	N	L	C	M	A	L	W	D	L	O	I	E
L	R	S	E	E	O	A	L	R	A	M	G	S	T	B
R	I	R	A	T	R	I	G	E	T	L	A	I	O	M
A	D	U	N	O	B	R	O	H	C	I	D	N	L	N
H	T	O	B	N	E	G	D	O	F	E	N	E	G	C
C	R	M	U	L	L	O	C	E	I	K	C	A	J	I

JACKIE COLLUM
ELMER SINGLETON
ROY WALKER
BILL HENRY
BILL BONHAM
RON TOMPKINS
LYNN NELSON
DICK LITTLEFIELD
GENE FODGE
LEFTY TYLER
MORRIE MARTIN
RAY NEWMAN
CHARLIE SMITH

79

```
O H T O S M A D A Y K R A P S
D A I L P O B E A R E D W L N
A O N A T i F L A M A Y E O J
S K N D H O E W M S N I T S I
N F I K L L T O E C N R O G T
E A Y G E E I E A A U R V T T
M L J A K S K H D B O T S I E
E D R E M R S C S B A O U N N
L O O S B E M I E T U B A D O
C W Z N M Y L V N A C B C Y B
G N R U D L E K I G J A W U O
U S K N E T E R C M E E G E I
O T I U S C I H N I T R K M L
D L F Z I X A Y W E D Z C A U
P L P A L O I G A R A G E O J
```

LINDY MCDANIEL
DON KESSINGER
JOEY AMALFITANO
STEVE BOROS
JULIO BONETTI
JAKE JAECKEL
JOE GARAGIOLA
DOUG CLEMENS
DICK LEMAY
ELLIS BURTON
SPARKY ADAMS

'60s Stylin'

```
E C A T D A L B K C I R S T O
T E L E G R A P E V O R G R F
T W T A I R E X C F E I R A J
E R J T R H A L S G O E I W I
D E M S E E B D D V T G C E M
R K O K H D N O Y H D K U T H
U A N D P O R C G H B R G S I
B B E E I E B U E O A A I Y C
E M R Z R G A M B J R T J M K
I O U D N L J S O Y O F T M M
D T N Y S T H U R N D N A I A
D A Y S C A B O A W R D E J N
E A S L W E S U M O S E E S E
R T A E U S A V E X I T O R D
F O T Y R O G E R G E E L S F
```

RICK BLADT
CLARENCE JONES
BOB SHAW
LEE GREGORY
FREDDIE BURDETTE
S. (STERLING) SLAUGHTER
JIM HICKMAN
GARY ROSS
TOM BAKER
JIMMY STEWART
ANDRE RODGERS
GRADY HATTON

Cubs

```
T S I V A D K C O R B I L S T
T H A N J O E K R E M O T N I
O E G R A O N I L A I O S I R
I D K I E R E B A S N L A L E
L B A A N L E S O Y A N G L Z
L U Y S R K B H T H T R A O Z
E M R O W D C A C R N I D H A
N P K A L R Y M T C A L I E L
E W E L M L I M M T D I V I Y
L I N O O L B T M I A S N S N
L L A R N D R I O A J P A S O
A L E O B U R K E I S A Y E T
T S H N O S N H O J E C N J L
E Q U N O S N H O J E C N A L
Y L L A N N O C E I Z T I R F
```

SAMMY DRAKE
JIM MCKNIGHT
PAT TABLER
JESSIE HOLLINS
BROCK DAVIS
FRITZIE CONNALLY
ALLEN ELLIOTT
JOE STRAIN
TONY TAYLOR
LEO BURKE
LANCE JOHNSON
TONY LAZZERI
BUMP WILLS

They Had the Stuff

R	Y	A	B	E	Z	H	E	T	W	O	S	F	V	M
A	D	O	N	R	T	P	U	O	R	T	E	L	I	A
Y	R	A	E	K	I	S	K	W	E	R	F	R	K	N
B	U	Y	N	S	E	U	R	V	G	E	K	E	I	T
U	L	A	R	N	R	O	E	I	C	C	N	M	S	E
R	B	A	G	K	Y	S	E	D	A	H	G	I	I	I
R	U	H	E	R	T	J	I	J	O	R	C	E	L	R
I	A	K	L	O	E	I	A	L	D	O	T	W	L	H
S	I	P	N	N	O	G	T	C	L	G	A	E	E	T
M	L	E	K	C	X	Z	M	A	K	E	V	K	M	U
E	T	I	I	S	M	E	L	A	L	S	M	A	I	G
K	N	M	B	A	X	C	O	N	D	J	O	J	J	K
S	T	A	N	C	U	Z	F	R	E	D	M	N	J	R
I	L	V	N	O	T	O	O	H	T	R	U	B	R	A
S	T	R	E	B	O	R	N	I	B	O	R	X	O	M

FERGIE JENKINS
JIM ELLIS
GREG MADDUX
KEN HOLTZMAN
STEVE STONE
JAKE WEIMER

ROBIN ROBERTS
MIKE KRUKOW
BURT HOOTON
DANNY JACKSON
RAY BURRIS
MARK GUTHRIE

The Cubbies Continue

Y	N	L	E	K	R	E	N	D	R	A	G	M	I	J
A	V	E	L	U	N	E	R	A	M	I	J	I	O	T
W	E	E	D	I	O	R	O	N	E	N	M	E	S	Y
N	A	I	L	U	C	I	E	G	A	G	O	D	E	R
E	R	C	O	L	I	E	A	H	A	V	A	R	B	E
W	Y	W	I	L	I	V	A	R	S	R	O	E	G	F
T	Y	T	R	A	A	V	D	F	N	U	O	T	I	E
K	I	M	O	S	W	E	N	O	B	O	B	R	H	L
I	S	A	D	O	N	A	L	A	R	U	G	O	Y	L
M	O	E	T	E	R	D	A	N	R	Y	O	U	B	I
B	T	C	R	E	E	H	O	J	O	A	K	T	R	K
A	P	E	D	A	T	I	G	L	O	N	M	E	I	L
L	O	B	R	A	C	U	D	L	E	R	F	R	K	L
L	E	L	Z	I	M	E	R	P	Y	L	L	I	B	I
E	Y	B	A	B	E	P	H	E	L	P	S	G	E	B

BILL KILLEFER
NEWT KIMBALL
R. (RABBIT) MARANVILLE
JIM GARDNER
BOBO NEWSOM
KIRBY HIGBE
TED SAVAGE
TY CLINE
BOB USHER
BABE PHELPS

How Was His Curve?

C	A	L	E	X	Y	B	I	C	H	R	O	D	M	O
Y	A	M	T	T	O	C	S	T	A	G	E	I	N	I
W	S	L	A	Y	T	E	I	R	E	D	K	I	N	N
A	L	T	V	E	R	M	C	T	D	E	O	D	A	J
A	J	L	R	I	S	V	D	I	M	T	S	M	O	I
M	I	F	E	E	N	G	E	A	P	M	F	H	L	M
K	M	D	V	W	B	S	S	U	I	F	N	H	O	K
A	E	A	C	R	O	O	C	T	O	G	E	Y	E	R
L	D	O	E	L	N	H	R	H	O	R	E	M	L	E
C	R	I	O	R	S	O	Y	E	I	X	E	S	O	M
R	O	M	E	E	P	U	T	A	V	R	I	C	L	M
G	O	U	I	H	G	Z	I	Z	J	A	A	N	O	E
N	P	Q	T	E	D	O	M	O	T	A	D	L	A	L
O	Z	E	R	E	P	S	I	K	R	O	Y	O	D	F
R	S	O	M	A	S	L	A	B	Y	N	O	T	G	I

JOHN GOETZ
EDDIE SOLOMON
DAVE ROBERTS
JAY HOWELL
CALVIN SCHIRALDI
YORKIS PEREZ
GUY HOFFMAN
JIM KREMMEL
TONY BALSAMO
SCOTT MAY
MIKE MASON
DAVE SMITH

Pitching Puzzles, Perhaps?

D	A	E	Y	E	L	I	R	E	G	R	O	E	G	K
C	I	D	A	V	E	C	O	L	E	C	Z	A	E	B
R	O	C	O	L	G	U	E	Q	D	E	N	I	M	S
U	R	E	K	D	M	N	T	I	V	I	T	A	O	H
S	I	D	N	S	H	F	C	V	O	R	C	R	A	B
S	Y	O	O	O	E	K	A	G	U	K	T	L	L	E
M	F	A	B	N	S	L	O	Y	S	A	M	O	L	D
E	O	B	W	E	E	R	M	T	M	A	S	R	E	K
Y	I	A	L	N	E	L	E	A	N	U	F	S	W	E
E	J	M	T	D	A	W	S	D	M	V	E	L	O	K
R	A	I	I	F	A	I	E	T	N	R	U	R	P	R
W	N	H	E	R	O	R	X	Y	O	A	I	R	L	I
E	I	R	T	R	S	N	B	H	E	N	B	T	L	S
P	D	A	F	E	M	A	N	D	E	T	S	O	I	T
D	D	U	L	L	I	D	U	A	C	L	L	I	B	Y

BILL POWELL
DICK SELMA
GEORGE RILEY
MACK STEWART
BOB ANDERSON
DAVE COLE
RUSS MEYER
BILL CAUDILL
DON ELSTON
GLEN HOBBIE
HAL MANDERS

A Mixture Through the Years

F	Z	T	I	M	H	C	S	Y	N	N	H	O	J	W
R	C	O	M	Z	R	E	T	R	A	C	L	U	A	P
A	X	I	T	E	N	E	A	R	E	G	O	B	Y	L
N	R	A	C	D	J	L	B	L	I	D	L	G	A	S
K	E	O	R	N	L	I	D	O	S	F	E	N	H	O
R	N	O	D	A	S	N	M	E	B	O	E	O	N	P
E	J	A	R	N	A	T	H	S	R	R	M	R	A	I
B	O	Y	O	R	E	G	E	G	T	E	U	U	I	C
E	E	Z	N	E	U	Y	E	V	L	V	L	S	E	K
R	B	E	T	H	R	D	M	R	E	C	R	T	H	A
G	L	B	M	O	E	A	O	Y	A	E	S	A	L	L
E	E	I	C	C	R	A	B	R	E	Y	N	N	I	L
R	J	V	K	I	C	I	T	C	O	R	U	G	S	N
I	N	E	T	H	A	E	S	L	I	F	S	O	E	B
E	R	N	U	C	R	A	P	A	W	T	I	L	A	L

PAUL CARTER
CHICO HERNANDEZ
FRANK REBERGER
JOHNNY SCHMITZ
GEORGE DECKER
JIM ST. VRAIN
MEL ROACH

JIM HUGHES
BOB RUSH
LEN RANDLE
RODNEY MYERS
STEVE ENGEL
AL LARY

Not Just Guys, Our Guys

M A Y C R E I P Y L L I B O C
G I L L O C S I R D Y D D A P
R I K Y R U R D R O I R D E Z
U C K E Y L C A T C O R T O E
O L F S J E E T K I I H L L L
B E S V W F R E R A L L A S A
H U R J N O R F N W U I D O Z
C H A R O I R G Y R Z O Y X N
I S E R C E A T E N O R D F O
R V O K O R K M S W N I A I G
E A S U R T Y P T O W O N P E
C O T E I N H L I V N T L E K
N O T J N U A D T B C H A R I
A T N E Y W O L J O I M O E M
L O L I R E S O T L A M I J S

MIKE GONZALEZ
LANCE RICHBOURG
LENNY MERULLO
WALT WOODS
ADRIAN GARRETT
JOHN OSTROWSKI
LONNY FREY
BILLY PIERCY
DICK ERICKSON
PADDY DRISCOLL
VERN FEAR

They Said, "Put That Lawnmower Away!"

```
D N E Y A R C I N E R R E Z S
S E N W H O Y I H V O T I A L
A L S O J T A E K E N B V E E
M E E D T O R L N M O I R Z A
M A N E I S M A P W H E N D H
A L L I T C N A C A O W A A C
R R T A I H K U L C I D N M I
G E E H C U O B D E M D M O M
X I G O B K R M A N C X E O H
E R E O A E N F A R O D E R P
L T B U E S I I L S T W L L L
A C T D T N A R U O M E A J A
F R E D R I C H A R D S L H R
R N W O R B Y M M O T I H L S
G A F P O K N I R B N O E L A
```

RALPH MICHAELS
LEON BRINKOPF
ALEX MCCARTHY
SHAWON DUNSTON
TOMMY BROWN
HAL BREEDEN
FRED RICHARDS
ALEX GRAMMAS
ED BOUCHEE
LEE THOMAS
DICK BARTELL

89

G	R	E	B	D	N	A	S	E	N	Y	R	E	R	O
A	N	T	T	E	P	I	R	O	C	M	R	Z	A	L
Y	E	V	D	E	Y	A	U	E	U	N	A	G	E	E
H	T	I	E	I	D	I	D	L	I	H	T	W	D	W
T	I	C	J	R	M	A	G	E	A	J	B	I	A	B
A	W	I	O	V	U	H	B	S	L	U	M	P	J	U
N	S	A	E	N	N	R	C	I	R	C	P	O	I	R
R	O	X	Y	E	O	L	I	S	S	B	H	T	G	D
E	R	U	K	G	A	C	E	Y	Y	N	E	A	O	E
B	U	D	L	N	I	T	D	I	F	D	A	Z	C	T
A	F	I	W	O	T	D	E	L	K	I	D	U	I	T
D	O	M	G	E	E	K	A	C	L	E	R	E	H	E
E	L	I	O	R	T	V	I	P	E	R	A	S	R	Y
T	E	V	F	B	I	L	L	Y	C	O	W	A	N	F
I	N	I	D	N	A	R	O	M	Y	E	K	C	I	M

MICKEY MORANDINI
LEW BURDETTE
BILLY COWAN
RYNE SANDBERG
ERNIE BROGLIO
TED ABERNATHY
JOHN FLAVIN
FREDDY SCHMIDT

A Clubhouse Collection

J	N	L	D	A	M	E	C	G	P	U	T	D	Z	Z
O	K	A	N	A	W	E	T	P	C	A	L	A	E	E
H	E	R	G	H	V	O	E	N	O	Z	A	N	D	U
N	T	O	E	E	K	E	K	A	J	R	I	B	N	G
B	I	G	V	L	H	A	S	F	C	T	W	D	A	I
O	H	R	A	F	L	M	E	T	R	P	W	K	N	R
T	W	E	I	I	O	I	I	A	E	Y	E	H	R	D
T	K	G	Y	J	C	K	M	J	H	V	R	I	E	O
A	C	G	G	N	A	Y	T	T	U	A	E	X	H	R
R	I	R	U	D	D	L	T	I	R	G	M	N	E	Y
I	R	O	A	N	E	B	A	B	V	U	S	B	S	R
N	R	S	A	F	N	O	M	T	E	C	K	I	O	N
I	E	S	E	N	I	L	C	E	N	E	G	M	J	E
P	D	R	E	N	T	T	I	B	Y	R	R	A	L	H
A	R	T	S	N	E	E	T	S	E	I	N	N	E	K

KENNIE STEENSTRA
KURT MILLER
HENRY RODRIGUEZ
JOSE HERNANDEZ
SANDY MARTINEZ
GREG GROSS
GENE CLINES
DAVE STEVENS
DERRICK WHITE
MATT MIESKE
JIM HEGAN
LARRY BITTNER
JOHN BOTTARINI

New Names Since the New Millennium

C	H	R	I	S	S	T	Y	N	E	S	W	A	S	T
S	O	I	H	S	I	R	T	C	I	V	C	E	N	I
A	K	R	H	E	I	W	A	O	T	E	R	M	A	M
M	B	E	E	C	C	W	H	T	E	F	S	I	A	G
L	U	K	N	Y	S	C	E	L	J	C	O	R	H	S
N	A	N	P	A	P	U	U	L	O	L	K	I	E	F
Y	O	R	Y	O	L	A	R	T	N	G	J	N	T	U
T	V	T	S	B	P	E	T	N	U	E	O	L	U	N
E	Y	E	R	H	E	E	I	T	O	J	R	O	D	I
R	E	I	S	U	Y	I	H	Z	E	D	A	R	T	X
H	A	O	Z	R	M	R	D	U	D	R	N	L	A	I
P	J	S	E	K	I	T	Q	D	O	U	S	E	R	D
N	T	S	O	E	C	C	T	D	E	O	R	O	L	W
O	X	O	F	D	A	H	C	A	I	R	Z	G	N	G
P	A	J	O	J	L	U	N	C	M	I	F	M	M	R

FREDDIE BYNUM
COREY PATTERSON
MARK GUTHRIE
GLENDON RUSCH
CHRIS STYNES
M. (MARK) GRUDZIELANEK
SCOTT EYRE
MATT MURTON
JOSH PAUL
JACQUE JONES
DARREN LEWIS
CHAD FOX

Didn't Throw Their Balls Back, Did We?

Y	H	T	T	N	O	W	E	N	E	D	A	N	A	O
G	R	M	X	O	C	Y	R	R	A	L	I	S	R	D
J	E	Z	M	M	D	A	V	E	S	O	C	T	R	A
E	U	O	E	A	R	D	I	J	U	S	T	E	A	N
R	L	O	R	R	R	A	Z	N	R	T	T	V	P	O
R	U	M	L	G	I	V	L	E	E	I	D	E	A	D
Y	F	P	A	A	E	M	E	Y	I	V	U	L	I	L
M	A	E	K	R	Y	B	A	L	O	L	T	A	C	A
U	L	D	E	C	K	D	E	R	W	S	E	K	R	M
M	A	G	L	I	N	P	A	L	S	Y	U	E	A	Y
P	Z	A	D	A	R	T	A	P	L	I	N	S	G	D
H	B	I	I	P	O	C	L	R	I	D	M	N	N	N
R	O	R	O	A	L	E	R	R	E	F	A	A	E	A
E	B	I	N	R	A	K	I	W	O	N	S	B	R	C
Y	T	Y	E	W	A	L	L	E	R	S	T	I	T	A

N. (NOMAR) GARCIAPARRA
MARK PARENT
CANDY MALDONADO
LARRY COX
MARVELL WYNNE
JERRY MUMPHREY
TODD ZEILE
ARAMIS RAMIREZ
TYE WALLER
GEORGE BELL
BRIAN DAYETT
STEVE LAKE

Bet They Dined At Ditka's

```
B R E L L I V N A L G G U O D
R I Y J O H N K O R O N K A O
N E C A V L Y S B E D O R C C
B I T K R O S E T G N E E E L
N R I S D R N C R I K O L W I
I A A U P G U E A L K R P K F
P L L D R M G M A R G W A G F
O M S I W S E W N A M L M B B
Y O E T M O D D R I D O I A A
T V T I N D O Y N A V L J R R
E H T R O W S D N A L L O H T
T H E T A C O I A L Y L A K O
W I L N O N E H O L E R N C S
O E C T U L F N A G L O H I H
D E T T S A G I R F R O N M H
```

CLIFF BARTOSH
GARY SCOTT
KAL DANIELS
BRAD WOODALL
CALVIN MURRAY
TODD WALKER
T. (TODD) HOLLANDSWORTH
GREG SMITH
BILL LONG
DOUG GLANVILLE
BEN GRIEVE
RYAN DEMPSTER
JOHN KORONKA

Addison Avenue Athletes

```
B R J A M I E X A R T I O N A
R I I O S A L Y A N N T H O L
O E I C H M R E P S O W R K L
S A T L K N A A M R D E R S E
H W I N L A N D E A D R E D S
T J E L O O G Y A N M R D T N
A O A R B M A U A E A C E V I
R S B O D D O X I B K R D I K
N E F Y A N E R Y L R I T C D
E A D B A L A A P Y E E M I A
W R O A A T Y E A S J R G R Y
O C S T D N W D N T A A A O E
N I T M N A A E P A R N C E W
D A I A N M M T L C H O E A E
M E M D S P A S I L R S P K D
```

RICK AGUILERA
TERRY ADAMS
MIKE ADAMS
RED ADAMS
KEN ASPROMONTE
TOBY ATWELL
SHANE ANDREWS
JOHNNY ABREGO
MATT ALEXANDER
JOSE ARCIA
MANNY AYBAR
DEWEY ADKINS

More Crazy Names

R	A	W	A	G	Y	P	P	I	H	C	Y	E	D	R
E	P	O	Y	A	K	L	U	R	I	N	A	M	I	E
D	E	K	N	B	I	R	E	L	A	G	A	G	E	S
I	M	O	E	T	M	L	K	M	I	H	G	H	K	A
E	I	O	R	T	L	O	R	W	A	S	S	D	R	D
Z	A	E	R	I	T	E	W	R	S	I	E	J	A	E
E	M	R	M	D	G	L	G	T	L	A	U	D	L	E
I	T	X	A	A	E	S	E	G	E	M	J	N	C	F
L	O	E	H	T	E	P	N	W	B	B	W	I	R	O
L	L	P	Z	H	H	E	K	O	I	O	A	S	E	N
O	I	O	C	E	Y	E	B	C	L	R	W	B	T	D
R	H	A	N	D	A	R	N	K	I	M	T	B	P	Y
Y	E	S	O	R	O	T	R	R	A	H	E	S	M	O
P	O	O	K	W	R	U	O	L	Y	O	C	G	U	R
N	W	O	N	E	T	R	Y	E	L	I	A	B	S	N

PEACHES GRAHAM
RIP HAGERMAN
JUMBO BROWN
RIGGS STEPHENSON
WOODY ENGLISH
SUMPTER CLARKE
S. (SWEETBREADS) BAILEY
KETTLE WIRTS
OX MILLER
TURK LOWN
DEE FONDY
ROLLIE ZEIDER
CHIPPY GAW

An Enlightened Year, 1988

L	E	P	A	C	E	K	I	M	I	S	H	U	G	S
G	C	S	T	O	S	E	D	R	T	D	O	N	A	E
E	R	V	Z	B	I	L	L	L	A	N	D	R	U	M
Z	J	E	W	A	H	X	A	R	R	I	O	F	R	O
E	E	L	B	A	Z	I	R	E	N	Z	O	J	E	O
N	F	Q	Y	D	L	A	I	Y	N	I	N	L	T	R
I	F	U	R	B	N	E	H	E	S	W	L	O	S	O
T	P	E	R	E	M	U	C	A	E	A	L	M	B	D
R	I	R	O	E	P	S	S	N	R	R	U	P	E	N
A	C	K	V	K	A	P	N	M	A	V	T	S	W	A
M	O	A	E	D	T	W	I	O	I	V	E	G	H	L
E	D	B	G	O	C	V	V	N	M	J	P	Y	C	O
V	R	U	O	F	L	I	L	J	L	D	E	D	T	R
A	O	P	I	N	N	D	A	Z	T	A	R	P	I	Z
D	A	N	O	R	W	K	C	I	R	A	D	F	M	I

MIKE CAPEL
BILL LANDRUM
CALVIN SCHIRALDI
ROLANDO ROOMES
JIM SUNDBERG
VANCE LAW
DOUG DASCENZO
ZAZA HARVEY
AL NIPPER
JEFF PICO
MITCH WEBSTER
RICK WRONA
DAVE MEIER
DAVE MARTINEZ

Supplemental Status Studs

N	S	H	T	I	M	S	E	I	L	R	A	H	C	L
O	I	N	B	K	T	O	B	Y	A	T	W	E	L	L
I	L	K	O	P	T	L	U	R	Z	C	M	E	L	Y
T	L	I	S	S	T	G	E	T	J	R	D	M	B	E
O	I	N	E	N	P	I	I	J	E	S	P	R	B	N
B	W	U	O	K	A	M	I	N	M	R	U	N	I	E
L	M	H	J	S	H	M	I	A	E	C	E	D	U	H
A	I	I	C	C	D	K	R	S	E	D	R	F	M	C
T	J	I	S	O	H	E	T	E	E	A	E	N	O	Y
B	V	B	Y	P	I	O	D	O	H	K	K	D	R	R
O	O	L	L	L	N	W	T	D	J	E	U	W	Y	R
B	E	A	L	W	A	J	U	S	G	F	N	D	R	A
S	R	I	A	R	H	B	P	R	I	F	N	E	A	L
U	W	R	D	O	O	G	R	U	B	L	I	W	G	O
A	D	S	B	C	Z	T	L	U	H	C	S	B	O	B

LARRY CHENEY
JIM DOYLE
WILBUR GOOD
BOB TALBOT
GENE HERMANSKI
WILLIE RAMSDELL
PRESTON WARD
JIM WILLIS
CHARLIE SMITH
VIC SAIER
BRUCE EDWARDS
BUD HARDIN
BOB SCHULTZ
TOBY ATWELL
DUKE SIMPSON
RALPH KINER

Some Of the Greats

```
H C H U C K T A N N E R N O J
C A S O S Y M M A S O E L O Y
A B R A H T I T O N E E E R B
B M A S E K N A S K D T I D S
U A N T R O B A C R I R N R N
E R S A M E N I E N O A H Y R
R K H B E T V U K A E V I A O
D R A W O H L E D D H U L T H
E G I L L B R I Y E C N O R S
E R K O A N A Z D N O C U O R
B A R C E I Z O L O N M I R E
E C H D N I S B O K E H T L G
B E C U D Y J I M M Y S O C O
M O R D E C A I B R O W N J R
R E D N A X E L A R E V O R G
```

ROGERS HORNSBY
RON CEY
VIC KEEN
MARK GRACE
MORDECAI BROWN
ED REULBACH
GROVER ALEXANDER

DIZZY DEAN
CHUCK TANNER
JOE TINKER
RON SANTO
SAMMY SOSA
DEL HOWARD
JOHNNY EVERS

50s Rockers & Rollers

```
B I J A C K S Y O N W H I L T
D E N A S T O B I C H A S R K
Y I H Y C O H E N E R F I Z A
B M X T I K E N K O R L E E G
R O T A R D L A R A M U C U A
A E B A I O R I N O G R J G N
E I R B E D W K T I S O R O R
K J I D Y H E S R T H A M S E
A N D L N M K D L N R E S H K
E X L U A A O N B L I E D U N
P O L G I R N R P R E T L M A
S P A X F T I H G E E K I L R
B I N A N G U R O A R O C L F
O R E D G O K E S J N A R I N
B V A S H T I M S L U A P D D
```

HY COHEN
SOLLY DRAKE
JOHN BRIGGS
BOBBY MORGAN
DICK ELLSWORTH
F. (FREDDY) RODRIGUEZ
JOHN ANDRE
BOB SPEAKE
JACK LITTRELL
PAUL SMITH
FRANK ERNAGA

With Ernie On Their Team, the Score Didn't Matter

S	C	A	I	V	E	R	N	M	O	R	G	A	N	H
I	D	H	F	N	I	S	D	B	E	C	N	G	T	T
Z	L	Y	A	V	O	S	I	K	A	O	I	O	S	L
U	E	N	L	R	D	S	A	W	N	N	N	U	R	T
T	I	B	O	E	L	B	L	N	Y	R	M	E	L	K
K	F	A	A	S	E	I	E	E	E	E	H	O	N	I
I	R	O	H	N	M	L	E	F	K	G	S	I	N	P
P	E	U	E	C	B	O	F	S	N	C	V	A	A	E
E	T	G	S	O	E	A	H	I	I	R	I	L	C	G
G	R	U	B	S	H	Y	K	T	I	L	L	M	O	R
R	O	L	T	C	M	M	P	E	Y	A	V	J	D	O
O	P	K	S	A	I	E	T	N	R	B	O	E	F	E
E	B	E	P	J	S	N	Y	Y	H	G	B	I	R	G
G	O	I	I	G	O	E	T	E	Y	O	K	O	N	A
J	B	T	O	M	I	X	A	O	R	B	J	I	B	O

JOE SCHAFFERNOTH
BOB PORTERFIELD
CHARLIE SILVERA
ED MICKELSON
BOBBY THOMSON
GEORGE PIKTUZIS
VERN MORGAN
AL LARY
JIM KING
RUSS MEYER
MONTE IRVIN
JOHN PYECHA
BOB LENNON
CASEY WISE

Should've Been Fine In '69

S	T	E	V	E	R	R	I	U	G	A	K	N	A	H
J	A	G	I	A	C	S	A	N	K	T	E	H	S	I
O	S	O	N	A	M	D	D	X	Y	I	S	H	A	W
H	H	D	T	O	R	L	K	O	N	S	P	A	T	E
N	I	O	N	G	S	O	E	O	N	L	F	W	E	S
N	T	J	S	O	F	N	A	S	O	Y	J	O	S	L
Y	A	R	O	C	M	Y	H	D	K	T	O	O	E	E
H	E	M	L	E	A	E	U	O	B	C	R	U	H	N
A	R	A	K	I	D	R	L	O	J	Y	I	V	N	O
I	D	Z	E	C	N	E	G	E	R	N	V	D	I	G
R	A	N	U	E	I	I	C	A	V	D	E	B	W	R
S	Z	O	K	H	C	H	G	K	M	A	I	K	E	A
T	I	M	A	P	L	C	M	O	E	B	D	O	N	H
O	L	E	D	A	C	R	C	I	U	R	L	R	O	A
N	I	K	T	I	S	A	R	I	J	O	L	E	E	M

KEN JOHNSON
JOHNNY HAIRSTON
KEN RUDOLPH
ARCHIE REYNOLDS
DAVE LEMONDS
HANK AGUIRRE
GARY ROSS
DICK SELMA
OSCAR GAMBLE
JIM HICKMAN
JOE DECKER
DON YOUNG

102

R	O	A	G	I	D	E	T	E	N	S	T	A	R	J
D	E	S	T	R	O	N	I	H	A	R	D	E	O	M
K	A	T	M	N	E	A	N	I	N	C	I	H	Y	L
I	T	R	S	A	A	B	E	R	H	P	N	E	H	O
L	M	R	R	U	I	M	N	S	S	N	R	T	U	H
T	O	L	A	E	H	L	D	E	Y	M	E	O	G	Y
R	N	H	I	W	L	C	L	O	D	W	F	U	H	L
U	E	C	A	V	E	L	S	I	O	N	K	R	E	L
N	Y	I	K	E	I	T	J	L	W	G	A	N	S	I
O	S	L	R	G	R	N	S	O	L	Y	L	V	A	B
P	T	R	L	O	R	A	G	K	H	I	E	A	Y	H
S	E	U	W	O	L	T	D	S	C	N	B	W	V	H
A	A	S	E	G	U	V	A	R	T	A	S	K	E	I
P	K	T	R	O	G	E	R	G	N	O	M	O	L	D
I	S	B	O	B	C	H	I	P	M	A	N	O	N	E

JOHNNY OSTROWSKI
BILL SCHUSTER
M. (MICKEY) LIVINGSTON
PAUL GILLESPIE
HY VANDENBERG
BILLY HOLM
HANK WYSE
IVAL GOODMAN
MACK STEWART
DEWEY WILLIAMS
ROY HUGHES
BOB CHIPMAN

Can You Remember From Back To 2001 Cubbies Odyssey?

```
D S Y Y D O O W N U D D D O T
E O C I T E V O W I E O J E R
L R D O S S D O K A R E O E K
I O E A T V R E B E T F Y B D
N N Y L H T I I S C R N R U R
O C A G L C C S A E H O M T O
D O R Y A E A H D T N C I C F
E O U A J F U M I C S N J I U
S M P H F I C M T A K T O S B
H E U F A G S O L R S U T I N
I R E A R N M M A L E S L A O
E J X I O E R A E Z I B O T M
L B F S R D O N U F L B O N A
D F A N O L L D F E R N V R D
S J M I C H A E L T U C K E R
```

SCOTT CHIASSON
ROBERT MACHADO
MICHAEL TUCKER
TODD DUNWOODY
FRED MCGRIFF
DELINO DESHIELDS
JEFF FASSERO
BILL MUELLER
JASON SMITH
RON COOMER
DAMON BUFORD
MATT STAIRS

Dudes!

I	T	S	E	R	G	M	H	O	L	D	A	N	O	R
Y	G	B	L	S	C	E	P	R	O	H	T	B	O	B
A	A	I	A	I	E	R	T	N	P	U	N	D	P	H
Y	L	N	S	R	A	H	K	O	T	E	N	A	T	O
L	E	H	T	J	E	A	M	S	V	E	U	I	P	R
O	W	N	O	U	I	C	A	H	I	L	R	E	K	E
R	A	F	I	S	E	M	T	R	M	D	D	A	R	G
P	D	P	E	A	J	U	F	O	N	E	O	E	A	C
E	E	R	B	O	R	N	S	A	F	H	T	H	C	A
K	R	E	N	K	E	K	L	E	N	B	L	E	V	M
I	C	E	C	W	A	E	C	O	Y	N	I	R	D	Y
M	S	I	O	U	I	N	D	U	S	T	I	O	B	D
R	D	G	J	B	A	D	K	Y	H	O	T	N	I	A
O	F	X	O	C	Y	R	R	A	L	C	N	I	G	R
T	A	H	A	R	G	E	S	H	E	I	M	E	R	B

SAM JONES
BOB THORPE
OWEN FRIEND
HOBIE LANDRITH
PAUL MOSKAU
DICK RUTHVEN
(ALAN) HARGESHEIMER

DON KAISER
JIM FANNING
GALE WADE
DON HOAK
CHUCK RAINEY
MIKE PROLY
LARRY COX

Memorable Names

```
O N A R B M A Z O D R A U D E
S N L S A D S A M J O N E S A
M T A R U H O L O S G P O W S
E B E R N D H E T E R A N N R
G R K V I C K A O P T G A V E
N A E T E M O V Y E B G A C M
A N N S A C A B D K A S T A M
R C S K K N H T O P L R O I U
T E M C Y A U R L L C G R R S
S X U S J R I E I A S O E I P
G B O O N R G W F S I F Z T M
U T E E V N P C U T T F E A A
O Y R E A M E N T O R M R S H
D O C E U W I J E S O N A O C
M A Z B A R R Y F O O T E S P
```

GEOVANY SOTO
ANGEL PAGAN
EDUARDO ZAMBRANO
STEVE CHRISTMAS
PORFI ALTAMIRANO
BARRY FOOTE
SAD SAM JONES
BUCK COATS
JOE KMAK
DOUG STRANGE
TED TURNER
BUMP WILLS
CHAMP SUMMERS

106

S	M	A	I	L	L	I	W	Y	L	L	I	B	X	O
I	L	S	K	N	A	B	E	I	N	R	E	N	U	W
C	Y	R	R	E	L	L	I	M	K	C	A	H	D	S
E	N	H	G	U	A	V	O	P	P	I	H	T	D	U
D	N	A	N	I	F	T	D	O	V	A	R	L	A	K
O	M	O	S	J	N	U	N	R	F	I	G	R	M	C
O	C	R	E	A	D	I	S	V	C	O	E	P	Y	O
W	G	L	S	E	M	A	S	H	N	S	R	E	R	L
Y	L	N	B	N	A	M	G	N	I	K	E	V	A	D
R	O	C	U	D	E	O	Y	G	I	F	A	E	G	A
R	T	G	E	W	S	O	N	S	H	A	Y	N	I	M
E	H	T	I	S	E	P	H	S	O	E	S	O	T	L
K	E	N	A	O	R	E	B	O	J	S	L	I	S	L
O	N	G	A	O	L	A	C	H	I	R	A	S	U	I
T	E	R	X	U	D	D	A	M	G	E	R	G	J	B

LYNN MCGLOTHEN
BILLY WILLIAMS
RON SANTO
GREG MADDUX
KERRY WOOD
HIPPO VAUGHN
DAVE KINGMAN
ERNIE BANKS
RICH GOSSAGE
BILL MADLOCK
SAMMY SOSA
HACK MILLER

So Many Years Ago

```
B R M A S Y D R A H X E L A G
O A C R I V A N E L L O R E Y
B X I A E N A R D O N A O K B
B I T D W L E O D E L R T A S
A R J A H E L W I V G O T L G
R D I Y C O S I E E O N O B I
R N M I T N N A M S E L M F R
E E G D U N S C U K A C C F G
T H A I B D C A L I C H G I R
T E R I C O K R L V L A S R E
M D D O N E D L I N O T H E V
B U N N E D A L G D E R F H N
A A E T O M S E A T O N R S E
R L R U S A S T N I C K O V D
L C S K O O R B Y D N A M L I
```

EDDIE MULLIGAN
GEORGE MCCONNELL
CLAUDE HENDRIX
BUTCH WEIS
HACK MILLER
ALEX HARDY
FRED GLADE
LES MANN
DENVER GRIGSBY
TOM SEATON
BOB BARRETT
SHERIFF BLAKE
MANDY BROOKS
JIM GARDNER

Forties' Fellas

M	U	S	O	Z	O	A	G	E	R	A	M	O	H	I
Z	L	R	E	D	D	I	E	W	A	T	K	U	S	Y
T	N	E	A	W	L	J	O	L	I	K	E	O	W	N
T	L	E	N	D	R	O	R	A	Y	M	R	O	S	R
O	C	M	H	R	J	O	G	O	B	E	R	E	R	E
I	H	S	P	C	I	D	E	H	T	O	K	R	E	N
R	R	S	R	O	S	C	H	O	B	E	E	A	U	G
R	I	U	V	W	S	K	E	K	N	D	L	Y	A	I
A	S	R	T	L	A	I	N	C	E	A	E	S	B	S
G	T	I	A	G	G	A	N	A	L	L	W	T	S	R
L	O	X	U	G	H	W	E	O	H	E	A	A	S	E
I	P	E	E	P	A	K	S	I	F	L	P	R	U	T
C	H	R	M	O	T	S	S	M	C	Y	D	R	R	L
E	E	Y	N	N	E	B	E	D	H	O	E	R	S	A
C	R	S	E	R	O	L	Y	B	O	D	T	A	R	W

GEORGE HENNESSEY
WALTER SIGNER
REGGIE OTERO
DOYLE LADE
TED PAWELEK
L. (LLOYD) CHRISTOPHER
HANK SCHENZ
HANK BOROWY
RAY STARR
RUSS BAUERS
RUSS MEERS
LEN RICE
CECIL GARRIOTT

Anyone Sound Familiar?

T B J E D E T E P N A D C W Y
H D I O R S C U A F A K D A D
S O R E H F I N L N O R P A E
I C R A L N O S N C A W N R K
Y M E V H O N Y U K J N Y L A
S E I E N R T Y C I Y P L T R
E L L E E A O E M M A A S E D
L K T G Y H H M U O D H A I Y
I E T L N S C R E N O R G M M
P R O B Y A P U A O L R R U M
H R S M N H M R O G M N E R A
A Z M A Y J T O R B D R G T S
P I N M G W L A T K D X O N F
J Y T A E Y C E D U M E H I D
E W A N Y E L A T S E L A G L

NEWT RANDALL
MEL KERR
TOM ANGLEY
JOHNNY MOORE
PETE NOONAN
SAMMY DRAKE
DANNY MURPHY
GALE STALEY
ED BOUCHEE
EARL GRACE
DANNY TAYLOR
MOE MORHARDT
JIM MCANANY
JIMMY SHECKARD

Still More Pitchers

P	I	X	S	A	H	B	S	A	K	P	U	D	Y	A
A	S	L	R	H	O	E	O	B	E	V	I	W	Y	D
U	G	R	L	B	A	A	R	H	Y	R	A	E	S	Z
L	R	N	E	A	T	W	G	B	I	N	L	E	M	T
E	E	R	R	P	R	K	N	U	B	K	Y	L	I	I
R	B	O	W	E	O	E	E	E	A	R	U	A	L	M
I	G	B	R	D	N	O	V	O	S	G	E	W	N	H
C	N	S	G	A	O	N	C	O	J	T	P	T	V	C
K	O	O	U	O	Y	Y	E	R	L	O	E	T	T	S
S	P	B	P	T	D	P	K	P	U	A	I	S	E	Y
O	S	O	J	N	C	A	I	I	N	B	V	H	I	N
N	L	B	A	D	U	F	M	E	L	E	L	R	C	N
A	R	H	I	B	I	T	H	O	R	N	K	I	O	H
T	A	I	J	E	R	O	S	M	E	C	F	K	W	O
E	C	B	O	N	I	V	R	A	G	D	E	N	E	J

MIKE CVENGROS
ORVAL OVERALL
CARL SPONGBERG
PAUL ERICKSON
JOHNNY SCHMITZ
RAY PIERCE
BOB OSBORN
KEN PENNER
SHAWN ESTES
NED GARVIN
HI BITHORN
HERB BRETT
WILBUR COOPER
ANDY COAKLEY

Hurlers

S	C	L	A	R	K	G	R	I	F	F	I	T	H	E
P	G	V	D	A	V	E	G	E	I	S	E	L	G	F
P	E	D	N	E	I	R	F	Y	N	N	A	D	L	O
A	O	D	I	K	L	N	F	O	U	S	I	L	L	P
U	R	N	P	R	O	Y	M	A	H	R	S	E	A	A
L	G	I	X	H	E	M	U	E	D	C	R	T	H	U
T	E	F	D	O	I	V	R	L	D	U	M	I	W	L
O	S	F	E	S	O	L	A	Y	B	A	N	K	E	C
T	T	I	T	J	N	C	C	E	R	Z	A	F	R	A
H	E	R	I	Y	I	T	K	A	W	E	T	F	D	R
E	U	G	N	V	T	R	E	B	R	Y	V	E	E	T
C	L	E	E	G	O	Y	E	M	Y	T	R	J	R	E
I	A	K	Z	H	C	O	L	O	I	B	E	R	O	R
L	N	I	G	V	A	N	R	E	W	O	C	R	A	T
L	D	M	T	H	A	K	I	M	R	B	I	D	E	H

VIC ALDRIDGE
PAUL TOTH
MIKE GRIFFIN
RUBE KROH
PAUL CARTER
CLARK GRIFFITH
GEORGE STUELAND

HARRY WEAVER
DAVE GEISEL
CURT SIMMONS
DREW HALL
LEFTY TYLER
DANNY FRIEND
LEFTY YORK

Talkin' Baseball

```
S D A F E W U T A R Z U J N O
A C A F R D N E O T A L O S F
R N O L Y G L Y R H S S N I R
Y K D T E C B E B E R O L R A
A P H Y T L U J R E E K E U N
N S Y D P W O G D A D Y I T C
D T G I E R I N R I I M C Z I
E O P K S O A L G A X E E I S
M W I B M Y A T L K M R S R B
P M S I M V E S T I U E T A E
S G T M E M V E C U A J E S L
T R I R A Z T V I F E M R E T
E J I Y R B A M N H O J S C R
R L O B L O R U A J N C H O A
L A T R O Y H A W K I N S I N
```

JIMMY ANDERSON
FRANCIS BELTRAN
RYAN DEMPSTER
LATROY HAWKINS
JON LEICESTER
SCOTT WILLIAMSON
CESAR IZTURIS
ANDY PRATT
MIKE WUERTZ
JOHN MABRY
DALE LONG
SERGIO MITRE
EARL AVERILL

At the Ol' Ball Game

U	E	W	A	R	R	U	H	C	S	E	N	Y	A	W
J	I	M	M	Y	L	A	V	E	N	D	E	R	I	A
I	K	X	T	I	B	E	G	U	T	E	J	H	C	J
T	Y	A	Z	E	K	S	U	R	R	O	J	G	O	O
T	L	Y	R	O	G	E	R	G	E	E	L	E	B	E
O	S	M	W	G	H	F	M	W	N	H	D	O	V	D
Z	M	C	A	B	N	P	A	I	T	T	B	R	U	M
Z	A	F	X	N	Q	L	G	I	T	F	O	G	L	C
A	I	E	I	U	L	E	M	O	I	C	P	E	A	D
M	L	T	E	I	F	S	C	S	B	A	H	P	B	O
A	L	R	S	Z	K	S	H	K	Y	L	A	E	E	N
R	I	S	H	C	K	E	C	E	R	U	M	A	L	A
B	W	V	I	C	R	T	P	H	R	K	G	R	I	L
O	Y	H	I	J	O	E	O	Y	A	E	O	C	D	D
B	C	D	D	N	A	R	O	M	L	R	N	E	K	C

LARRY BITTNER
BOB RAMAZZOTTI
BOB FISHER
CY WILLIAMS
JOE WALLIS
WAYNE SCHURR
JIMMY LAVENDER
MIKE MITCHELL
GEORGE PEARCE
ED MCDONALD
LEE GREGORY
DICK SCOTT

Here Are 15 Good Names

```
I M E L Y R O G Y N N H O J T
G W I K O N O I T A N Y E O J
N M I K E M A H O N E Y S S O
I O I L E N A L W O V M M H R
D R D S L W E B U C A E A A Y
L T E E M I A E D R C V D N L
A E O N V A E L K B E I A E J
R O E N N E E G K O L H Y A E
P R A W Y A U L R E T N B N S
S E T H A T T Q V E R O B D S
Y M A C H L A K N A E D O R F
R I G R W A L Y C E L N B E R
R N I T U H O S L U B D E W E
E E O P P I G R O O H U E S E
J E F F R E E D F R R C R Z D
```

MARK GUTHRIE
RUBEN QUEVEDO
JERRY SPRALDIN
MIKE MAHONEY
WILLIE GREENE
LEE WALLS
TONY TAYLOR
BOBBY ADAMS
JOEY NATION
JEFF REED
ISMAEL VALDEZ
SHANE ANDREWS
MIKE WALKER
CHUCK TANNER
JOHNNY GORYL

Itching To Play

```
N O S R E T T A P E I G G E R
K E D D I E S T A C K E N A D
M C I A S H I V E S E R T O R
E I I K C O U R T E S S K I A
A E C R N L Y E N O I F N L B
D U R K R O V E K T O M A G B
R I L Y K E R O A V E D U I U
E O Y E T E D B U S T E R V H
H X I R I L L D N G O M R O E
E D O K I E R L U A H A N L K
L U E S U T I A E A M N G E I
T H U G O O P U E H L R I O M
B H I N E R H E I M E C E J S
O M T S I V A D K C O R B H S
D I E N O Z N A F N E M R A C
```

JOE LOVIGLIO
REGGIE PATTERSON
MIKE HUBBARD
EDDIE STACK
HERMAN BRONKIE
CARMEN FANZONE
BROCK DAVIS
STEVE TROUT
MIGUEL BATISTA
EARL TYREE
MICK KELLEHER
CLAUD DERRICK

Not Much Time With the Cubs Here

N	I	P	A	C	Y	E	H	T	R	O	N	N	O	R
S	D	R	A	W	D	E	K	N	A	H	O	S	E	E
R	E	R	E	N	N	E	P	N	E	K	R	L	Z	T
N	N	M	E	Z	V	O	I	D	R	E	T	C	T	H
O	E	K	I	K	E	N	T	H	Y	S	O	H	I	C
S	D	S	O	R	L	A	K	E	R	B	M	I	V	I
N	I	D	J	O	G	A	M	A	S	E	M	C	O	R
H	R	O	V	A	H	H	W	P	T	W	Y	K	E	E
O	R	O	G	H	C	T	G	Y	U	I	O	S	I	I
J	O	W	I	I	I	K	L	I	R	C	R	M	N	G
F	C	T	R	B	H	J	R	A	E	R	T	I	R	G
F	D	L	B	L	R	T	A	O	W	L	A	T	E	E
I	E	A	I	C	A	D	O	C	W	B	R	H	F	R
L	R	W	N	N	E	P	N	E	K	A	L	U	E	O
C	Y	S	L	A	P	N	I	C	K	A	N	M	B	N

ERNIE OVITZ
JACK ROWAN
RON NORTHEY
HARRY WALKER
RICH MEYERS
RABBIT WARSTLER
BURLEIGH GRIMES
REGGIE RICHTER
CY SLAPNICKA
HANK EDWARDS
KEN PENNER
RED CORRIDEN
WALT WOODS
CLIFF JOHNSON

And a Bit Of Pine Tar

```
N I Y K S W O B A R D E O M K
E O G N A N S O R B M I J E T
A J T O D D P R A T T I N W O
T E H N Y O G R U H N T A S M
E R T R R A S J A C B L K U L
R R S U A O D E O O T I O G U
R Y T O P T H N T M A C A N N
E K A T L R T T O R D K C I D
S I L F I L E R E M P O H K S
I N F O R N Y M A R K N O M T
A D R W F N A D T L D C W I E
K A B I E Z C E R B Y N I J D
N L E C H R I S W A R D A R T
O L S I V A D M I J K A S I D
D K T N A N E S I H W E T E P
```

DICK DROTT
KENT BOTTENFIELD
TOM LUNDSTEDT
ANDRE THORNTON
PETE WHISENANT
SOLLY DRAKE
JIM DAVIS
MOE DRABOWSKY

TODD PRATT
RICK MONDAY
CHRIS WARD
WALT MORYN
JIM KING
DON KAISER
JIM BROSNAN
JERRY KINDALL

Wait! There's More

H	G	U	A	B	Z	T	R	A	W	S	E	V	A	D
N	A	M	G	N	I	L	C	Y	L	L	I	B	M	B
N	E	R	M	I	D	N	O	S	S	A	T	A	I	K
O	E	J	R	K	E	V	E	N	O	R	T	L	L	E
G	R	E	I	Y	A	F	E	N	C	T	L	R	O	Y
I	O	N	R	M	W	D	A	N	K	L	C	E	M	E
G	L	M	A	G	E	O	I	I	E	C	P	U	A	L
M	Y	B	A	M	D	L	L	E	L	A	I	C	Y	D
R	A	E	O	I	D	R	L	V	A	E	R	D	H	A
O	T	T	E	V	O	U	A	I	E	D	E	C	A	R
N	K	S	P	Y	G	L	A	W	S	R	I	E	W	B
O	C	A	L	M	U	N	S	R	D	R	T	M	L	L
S	A	R	E	O	F	G	W	Y	B	E	N	O	J	L
T	Z	L	E	Z	N	A	G	N	H	O	J	I	N	I
R	E	U	A	N	E	F	E	I	T	Y	B	B	O	B

TOM EDENS
DAVE SWARTZBAUGH
BOBBY TIEFENAUER
BOB RAUDMAN
NORM GIGON
EDWARD GREEN
HARRY WOLVERTON
BILL BRADLEY
JIM ELLIS
BILL LEE
LEE ELIA
ZACK TAYLOR
DICK NEN
MATT KILROY
JOHN GANZEL
BILLY CLINGMAN

119

J	H	T	I	M	S	Y	E	L	R	A	H	C	Z	C
O	I	S	H	A	N	K	G	R	A	M	P	P	O	E
Z	R	M	T	H	A	O	N	K	Y	P	R	U	L	N
N	E	P	B	E	J	I	S	C	G	A	H	R	T	R
N	T	L	T	R	V	O	R	Y	P	I	I	E	L	O
T	I	Y	A	L	I	E	H	E	T	H	A	W	E	B
F	C	T	S	Z	I	L	M	N	T	E	N	A	M	S
O	H	J	R	P	N	D	L	A	C	M	K	L	Y	O
K	M	E	L	A	W	O	E	H	C	H	O	I	U	B
C	R	L	N	R	M	H	G	D	E	K	U	T	M	O
E	I	B	A	T	F	C	D	E	C	A	O	R	S	B
B	B	A	R	T	R	E	J	R	K	A	R	O	R	A
F	A	L	I	D	O	A	R	F	U	I	J	T	D	Y
H	C	L	E	W	Y	N	N	H	O	J	M	I	K	E
I	C	H	T	I	F	F	I	R	G	Y	M	M	O	T

HANK GRAMPP
MIKE TYSON
CHARLEY SMITH
MIKE GONZALEZ
JIM BRILLHEART
RALPH MICHAELS
JOHN CHURRY
ART NEHF
STEVE MACKO
J. C. MARTIN
TOMMY GRIFFITH
BILL PIERCY
JOHNNY WELCH
FRED HANEY
BOB OSBORN

Put That Lawn Mower Away

Y	S	A	M	M	A	R	G	X	E	L	A	B	I	T
I	O	H	L	U	R	T	O	L	O	L	K	H	A	J
F	R	T	I	M	A	Y	E	D	E	C	A	Z	S	T
N	P	G	H	F	L	E	H	X	J	L	T	L	K	R
O	O	O	S	G	T	A	M	O	B	I	E	T	Y	A
S	U	R	K	H	I	C	L	R	W	A	P	S	E	W
A	S	B	O	N	C	N	E	E	H	V	E	O	X	E
J	T	M	U	A	I	E	K	C	D	E	R	H	T	T
A	A	F	R	E	D	R	I	C	H	A	R	D	S	S
S	G	T	R	E	A	M	B	C	M	Y	E	A	T	Y
T	H	E	N	B	H	E	U	N	O	M	E	M	L	M
Y	S	F	A	P	O	O	L	D	O	Y	I	I	R	M
I	M	R	L	G	B	I	D	E	W	E	N	J	S	I
T	G	A	V	D	M	U	W	E	F	I	L	I	T	J
B	R	Y	E	N	W	O	D	M	O	T	E	M	E	M

LEON BRINKOPF
ALEX MCCARTHY
HAL BREEDEN
ALEX GRAMMAS
JIMMY STEWART
B. (BILLY) GRABARKEWITZ
FRED RICHARDS
JIM MCKNIGHT
RALPH MICHAELS
ED BOUCHEE
LEE THOMAS
TOM DOWNEY

Put Me In, Coach

```
T D P I D E F A C H C S O T E
S A P A U B L O R U C N G S S
P N S N A G O L B O B O N R T
I I A I N D M O T O R R I U A
L E I G V I R T B D S E J H R
L L F O R A D A O A D Z A N I
I G E N T O D N W M I V M O E
H A T R W H M T A K W E E D J
P R H N C A K Y R T C A S I A
R I S F S R E A B U O I M H C
O B W S G R E D U B C W D R K
L A A R Y K S L O H O P M O T
Y Y E B O M A R I O L B A N O
A I T Y H S E W D R A T S W N
T S R E D N A S T T O C S O Y
```

GORDON MASSA
JIM WOODS
TOM POHOLSKY
DANIEL GARIBAY
TAYLOR PHILLIPS
DICK WARD
CURT DAVIS
BOBBY MORGAN
ED MAYER
SCOTT DOWNS
SCOTT SANDERS
DON HURST
BOB LOGAN

Windy City Winners

D	I	G	G	O	R	B	E	T	U	M	A	K	I	R
S	E	T	H	R	I	D	G	E	W	A	E	J	I	K
P	R	N	C	A	Y	D	E	G	A	R	R	C	O	L
R	N	A	N	U	D	N	O	M	O	E	K	T	E	L
E	N	S	C	I	H	T	H	O	H	S	T	I	E	T
Y	O	I	D	A	S	I	M	C	U	O	B	R	D	O
E	X	E	S	T	I	E	T	T	V	U	O	M	A	D
M	I	V	E	E	I	A	C	O	D	M	I	R	V	D
H	D	A	P	N	H	L	G	K	E	K	V	O	E	H
C	W	D	N	Y	I	E	N	Z	E	I	M	B	Y	U
T	A	O	L	F	L	O	I	V	Y	R	C	E	L	N
U	D	L	F	I	M	S	A	P	G	L	S	L	O	D
D	I	E	V	L	D	I	D	K	E	L	O	L	P	L
B	P	E	J	E	L	F	F	E	G	I	T	E	E	E
E	N	E	T	M	O	L	Y	K	U	B	V	S	S	Y

DUTCH MEYER
DENNIS ECKERSLEY
RICK SUTCLIFFE
DAVEY LOPES
MONK DUBIEL
TED SIZEMORE
BILLY HATCHER
MIKE VAIL
OTTO VOGEL
TODD HUNDLEY
DONNIE MOORE

Remember Any Of These Guys?

```
K E N N Y B E H S E S V M E N
B B R E T B A R B E R I E K B
Z U A C K I N T D H K O E R R
E M D C D F G L C E H Z P E A
M Z S D N M A Z H P S E H Y N
O A I P Y V L U A A E S A S T
G T M J O S B O M M I E R A B
O S S R E B C L P W O R S N R
E R D M A V E H S A A G W C O
L E R R E T I E U O M H O H W
P E D I S L V N M L W H T E N
U T E K C E J Y M I T O C Z L
T N C I T A C R E V I Z D L A
N I D S D A V E R O S E L L O
R T R E P M U H S Y R R E T E
```

BUDDY SCHULTZ
RICK STELMASZEK
DAVE ROSELLO
MIKE HUBBARD
BRANT BROWN
TERRY SHUMPERT

REY SANCHEZ
STEVE SWISHER
CHAMP SUMMERS
BRET BARBERIE
LEO GOMEZ
PEDRO VALDES

On the List

F	M	S	W	A	Y	Z	A	X	F	I	Y	B	O	E
E	R	I	K	P	A	P	P	A	S	O	C	K	L	M
S	C	A	N	M	L	I	V	M	R	A	T	H	L	N
E	O	V	N	R	F	E	L	L	I	B	S	O	E	A
S	N	I	W	K	I	S	E	S	M	R	B	T	S	M
G	W	N	E	D	C	C	S	I	K	N	M	L	O	H
N	F	O	C	I	M	A	K	O	A	A	F	E	R	O
O	E	M	K	K	R	E	S	W	R	K	O	R	E	L
L	O	R	C	U	P	H	I	T	I	G	E	P	V	L
V	J	U	V	E	R	D	Y	E	I	L	G	R	A	I
U	H	P	R	O	W	K	T	F	I	L	K	E	D	W
C	T	E	B	G	E	A	E	H	E	E	L	I	R	F
R	Z	S	L	O	U	D	H	K	G	K	T	O	N	G
A	D	T	U	I	R	X	T	M	I	J	I	V	D	S
W	O	G	M	A	H	S	R	C	P	M	O	M	I	Z

CHUCK MCELROY
ERIK PAPPAS
MIKE FYHRIE
DAVE ROSELLO
GREG GROSS
FRANK CASTILLO
RICK WILKINS
WILL OHMAN
MIKE KRUKOW
MIKE PEREZ

War Years Line-Up

C	A	J	D	Y	E	D	Z	O	N	R	E	W	C	K
C	H	N	O	C	R	R	O	Y	H	U	G	H	E	S
B	U	A	N	H	I	O	R	D	O	J	I	H	J	O
K	I	L	R	O	N	U	C	D	O	C	F	N	N	L
N	Y	L	C	L	S	N	K	E	O	G	N	R	N	F
W	O	I	L	P	I	R	Y	H	S	Y	C	A	A	G
D	C	S	B	S	O	E	E	M	L	K	C	E	M	D
O	M	G	N	Y	C	R	G	D	O	A	N	M	H	O
N	F	I	Y	H	N	H	E	A	L	O	C	A	T	E
A	O	N	R	A	O	R	U	K	S	A	R	J	R	I
L	O	L	N	P	T	J	H	S	N	S	E	E	A	F
T	B	D	B	F	Y	S	N	A	T	U	A	L	G	N
O	E	E	M	A	A	A	U	O	R	E	P	W	A	S
Z	B	E	K	S	W	E	R	S	D	U	R	L	A	D
I	S	A	L	L	E	M	O	C	E	G	R	O	J	Y

DALE ALDERSON
CHICO HERNANDEZ
CHARLIE GASSAWAY
FRANK SECORY
JORGE COMELLAS
DON JOHNSON
RAY PRIM
TONY YORK
BILL SCHUSTER
ROY HUGHES
GARTH MANN
JOHNNY MOORE
RED LYNN

126

J	O	S	E	F	H	I	E	N	A	D	I	O	Z	N
C	J	O	S	E	U	K	A	N	K	J	L	I	R	A
B	N	J	H	I	J	M	I	L	O	A	T	A	L	M
M	O	D	O	S	E	L	M	S	N	R	M	N	K	Z
O	P	E	D	S	O	J	E	E	O	J	O	S	E	U
W	P	S	N	M	E	N	D	E	U	S	J	O	S	G
E	H	R	E	J	U	R	S	V	A	T	P	C	O	E
S	I	S	M	N	A	O	E	I	O	W	O	O	J	S
O	O	U	E	C	J	A	C	Y	O	S	T	B	M	O
J	L	Z	E	D	N	A	N	R	E	H	E	S	O	J
S	T	S	I	I	M	T	E	S	O	S	H	I	P	J
O	O	F	G	E	H	F	I	D	E	S	O	J	L	E
J	R	P	S	O	J	O	S	E	T	A	V	A	R	O
I	E	O	N	I	A	C	Z	I	V	E	S	O	J	A
S	J	O	S	E	B	A	U	T	I	S	T	A	O	B

JOSE HERNANDEZ
JOSE MOLINA
JOSE GUZMAN
JOSE CARDENAL
JOSE NUNEZ

JOSE MACIAS
JOSE BAUTISTA
JOSE VIZCAINO
JOSE ORTIZ
JOSE REYES

They Did the Job

G	A	M	U	L	S	I	V	A	D	Y	D	O	J	S
M	O	N	T	P	G	A	W	O	B	Y	R	R	A	L
D	U	N	H	I	G	T	C	D	K	O	N	G	D	K
I	N	K	R	R	I	V	R	O	E	D	O	N	R	C
C	R	L	B	U	R	I	B	F	N	D	A	I	E	I
K	D	I	C	K	B	E	R	T	E	L	L	J	G	W
I	N	I	A	G	N	H	L	K	E	I	E	Z	N	T
E	E	P	U	D	H	E	S	R	M	R	T	R	I	S
N	Y	O	A	E	O	W	O	A	S	I	S	C	L	A
O	D	X	M	V	J	M	P	D	E	A	D	O	L	E
L	S	T	A	R	H	O	H	R	C	I	A	R	U	Y
E	E	V	U	T	N	S	N	W	I	E	H	W	B	L
S	A	P	I	C	X	E	O	N	I	G	D	C	M	W
T	F	E	B	E	K	E	T	A	Z	F	I	S	I	A
E	K	K	A	I	N	E	C	N	I	W	D	E	J	R

KEITH MORELAND
JODY DAVIS
RAWLY EASTWICK
LARRY BOWA
RICHIE ASHBURN
ED WINCENIAK
KEN REITZ
DOUG BIRD
DICKIE NOLES
DICK BERTELL
JIM BULLINGER
JOHN BRIGGS

Never Forget Your Teammates

T	L	A	S	N	I	G	G	O	C	K	N	A	R	F
Z	S	A	L	M	O	N	T	R	E	U	I	L	R	P
E	E	U	T	S	D	E	I	W	E	A	R	A	E	I
D	T	U	B	S	A	N	T	H	R	P	N	T	W	O
N	A	N	Q	E	U	N	T	T	H	K	E	T	A	L
A	S	L	N	R	O	R	S	E	C	L	O	W	L	L
N	S	U	R	O	A	H	R	O	A	J	T	R	L	E
R	U	A	O	E	A	M	P	C	I	H	I	A	Y	S
E	R	P	I	M	K	E	O	M	E	C	O	N	M	O
F	A	E	S	O	D	C	T	L	O	I	W	P	O	R
K	L	K	D	I	K	Y	O	C	A	T	M	I	R	E
N	Y	I	S	A	R	M	A	L	H	Z	E	A	N	V
A	N	M	Y	O	C	R	I	K	B	E	N	V	S	A
R	O	U	N	W	T	A	A	N	T	O	R	O	E	D
F	T	E	A	Y	S	D	U	S	D	R	B	W	G	E

TOM PHOEBUS
TONY LARUSSA
ART SHAMSKY
GONZALO MARQUEZ
FRANK FERNANDEZ
PETE LACOCK
RICO CARTY
MIKE PAUL
FRANK COGGINS
AL MONTREUIL
BOB LOCKER
DAVE ROSELLO
JIM TYRONE

129

```
S T A Y E N O L A M Y L L I B
B E L R Y B E E L Y U D O N T
O N D U T L K N O L N R Z K Y
C O N O X I L E B A E E M B V
A L A W N G L E L C D B S A I
J A P A T W D T K N S G S G J
R M N B M O E N A E I N E E O
E T N J N E M N R R G A R K L
M A O P W O R L G A R R H A E
L P D S D E Y R I E Y C O R M
E L S K H T E T L W R M I E D
L E N E V V I A H F T T A R G
L O S J N E X I P V T L Z C A
Y O N E S I T A T N O M A R K
J E D R U E P R E S T O M W E
```

PAT MALONE
GEORGE KELLY
LES SWEETLAND
JOSE HERNANDEZ
DENVER GRIGSBY
JERRY WHITE
WALT WILMOT
LES BELL
BILLY MALONEY
ELMER JACOBS
RAMON TATIS
DON WENGERT
RAY MACK

Wrigley Fielders

A	T	I	K	O	I	L	G	I	V	O	L	Y	A	J
T	N	O	G	O	R	A	N	I	L	O	M	B	O	B
L	N	O	S	R	A	L	N	A	D	M	B	D	Y	R
O	L	I	S	G	C	I	X	G	I	R	P	E	E	E
U	N	E	F	R	G	U	R	K	E	N	E	G	L	H
S	T	I	W	F	E	I	E	L	K	M	T	K	S	C
H	J	R	E	H	I	D	R	E	K	L	O	E	O	T
Z	O	E	S	T	I	R	N	B	M	K	Y	T	B	E
E	A	D	V	A	S	K	G	E	N	A	R	V	D	L
O	Y	N	Z	O	R	Y	L	E	H	A	C	F	A	F
R	N	I	G	A	P	H	D	L	K	E	D	I	H	T
G	D	C	V	H	A	S	L	N	J	I	V	C	T	T
E	U	E	Y	L	N	I	N	M	A	S	M	E	Y	O
T	C	T	L	R	B	I	R	B	U	R	S	A	T	C
W	A	Y	N	E	N	O	R	D	H	A	G	E	N	S

MIKE GRIFFIN
SCOTT FLETCHER
STEVE HENDERSON
DAN LARSON
DAN BRIGGS
JAY LOVIGLIO
WAYNE NORDHAGEN
BILL HAYES
MEL HALL
GENE KRUG
RANDY STEIN
BOB MOLINARO
MIKE DIAZ
THAD BOSLEY

The Northsiders

```
T O G L A V L E W R I C H I E
T E G U L C E W I D U T E F U
G R B T R H O S I N R M N A G
R O A E Z K U P O E N A O Y E
E A S D E B Y B Y A W R L B O
B N A T E B A T B L E V A O R
I F W I S R D Y R O K R M T G
R L I O R T H E A A B I T U E
F R A A R I C O R H M C A B B
E I G A R B E T R F A K P R R
I A C K O N Y T V N Y E U E O
N A U L H N G A S T E R I S W
R D O G S H T O R P A T M K N
E S M A I L L A I W O T T O E
B I F F A R M I K E K A H O E
```

FRED BEEBE
MARTY KRUG
GEORGE BROWNE
MIKE KAHOE
TRADER HORNE
CUNO BARRAGAN
OTTO WILLIAMS
MARV RICKERT
BERNIE FRIBERG
RAY BROWN
PAT MALONE
LEW RICHIE
BOB BUHL

For the Cubs

```
C N O S N H O J F F I L C R Y
L A E T L U H C S K N A R F U
I M A N D Y B R O O K S R F T
F E T O O F Y R R A B A R O E
O E S H E P R A L L N S E M L
R R B K O A Y E S K C E V I D
A F C U A M E Y D D E T A R N
N K I D C M B E O M F I H T A
I C R G A K M T O S E R N C R
L U A G D A H E W B E R E A Y
O B E O A S T E Y H N I K N N
M E L R A Y C A R T M I J L N
B X I D N E W N A Z O D B T E
O S T A N H E M G A O T R U L
B I S E V E E H C L I G R I V
```

BARRY FOOTE
BOB MOLINARO
LENNY RANDLE
FRANK SCHULTE
FRANK DEMARAIS
LEE MAGEE
VIRGIL CHEEVES

JIM TRACY
GARY WOODS
CLIFF JOHNSON
FRED MERKLE
BUCK HERZOG
BUCK FREEMAN
MANDY BROOKS

Not So Long Ago

R	E	Y	E	M	E	L	L	E	W	D	D	O	T	R
P	J	E	N	R	I	Q	U	E	W	I	L	S	O	N
L	E	N	K	O	C	T	I	N	I	R	E	T	J	A
N	R	J	O	B	U	C	E	V	O	C	K	O	O	R
I	O	Y	C	T	O	Y	N	G	E	R	H	I	D	S
A	M	C	A	D	S	B	R	K	Z	N	L	R	E	I
L	Y	H	J	N	A	R	H	K	K	E	U	E	Y	O
C	B	A	O	D	O	Z	I	O	U	H	B	H	A	B
C	U	R	S	F	A	M	R	A	W	K	I	T	N	U
M	R	M	E	R	M	O	A	W	H	R	E	N	I	D
T	N	L	H	A	N	G	I	L	I	Y	Y	A	E	N
T	I	E	P	K	E	O	T	A	L	S	R	Y	J	O
O	T	S	A	W	U	F	I	H	B	E	O	R	R	S
C	Z	E	R	Y	E	T	T	O	C	S	Y	I	E	A
S	O	R	A	V	A	N	E	R	U	B	N	A	V	J

TODD WELLEMEYER
JERRY HAIRSTON, JR.
JEROMY BURNITZ
RYAN THERIOT
BOB HOWRY
RYAN O'MALLEY
J. (JERMAINE) VAN BUREN
JOHN KORONKA
JASON DUBOIS
ENRIQUE WILSON
SCOTT MCCLAIN
SCOTT EYRE
JAE KUK RYU

What Size Shoe, I Wonder?

```
S K J A T S O W I G R O S E W
G J A S T I N P R U V M I H I
C A U G A W O E B E A R T I L
N Y R N E I D D E D T E E P L
A J A Y I R I C A B L H K P I
M O Y M W O R L T E F S A O A
T H H U X O R A C A R I L V M
R N E L E A O K C A L F X A M
O S R E K I C D E V A B D U O
W T A K U O D E S N L O E G R
K O L I F M E C M I N B A H S
C N D M A H R U D N O E L N K
U E D O N N I R H G I W D R O
H O N O T N E B H C T U B Y F
C E G D I R D N A T S E T E P
```

GARY WOODS
LEON DURHAM
HIPPO VAUGHN
BOB FISHER
PETE STANDRIDGE
CHUCK WORTMAN
MIKE LUM
JUNIOR KENNEDY
BUTCH BENTON
KARL ADAMS
MAX FLACK
JAY JOHNSTONE

Infield Groundskeepers

Y	R	A	Z	K	C	A	M	O	W	Y	N	O	T	H
S	I	N	C	G	C	P	L	U	M	E	R	F	O	W
S	T	E	A	N	O	H	U	P	T	I	H	W	T	I
E	B	B	M	L	F	I	O	N	A	R	A	C	T	L
M	Z	A	O	E	E	L	R	A	F	R	Z	H	O	L
O	W	P	N	O	D	H	E	G	D	E	V	U	K	Y
D	E	R	U	N	E	O	P	F	B	L	S	T	N	E
X	D	E	P	J	I	D	R	T	C	T	K	O	A	I
I	O	S	L	U	C	E	E	N	R	B	U	L	B	N
W	C	O	E	M	I	R	G	I	I	A	R	N	E	K
E	C	E	K	G	R	P	N	D	X	O	W	E	V	D
Y	A	V	A	Y	I	G	J	O	E	A	R	S	D	O
I	S	U	Y	T	E	P	B	R	S	A	T	U	A	L
N	E	N	E	R	O	O	M	Y	E	L	R	A	H	C
E	Y	E	N	O	O	C	Y	M	M	I	J	I	T	I

TONY WOMACK
HOWARD FREIGAU
ZEB TERRY
ART PHELAN
OTTO KNABE
LOU STRINGER
JIMMY COONEY
DOC CASEY
CHARLEY MOORE

Liver & Onions & These Guys

T	A	T	R	E	N	R	A	W	S	K	O	O	H	D
O	O	H	I	N	I	R	O	T	C	V	U	T	O	N
T	L	N	B	I	L	L	P	I	E	R	C	Y	R	O
T	Y	F	Y	L	R	O	W	E	C	N	F	B	A	S
O	T	A	E	K	R	R	C	M	U	R	U	A	G	T
V	R	O	O	L	A	H	G	A	E	C	F	M	H	R
O	B	I	I	W	M	U	U	D	K	N	E	R	I	E
G	N	L	L	L	S	E	F	F	A	Y	H	D	C	B
E	I	R	V	C	L	U	R	M	R	B	E	C	E	O
L	A	L	Y	G	S	E	B	J	A	A	G	O	D	R
C	T	O	H	S	E	U	N	M	A	N	C	T	S	E
P	S	E	E	M	L	T	D	E	X	C	N	S	E	V
U	S	L	A	J	I	E	M	K	L	E	O	K	O	A
R	L	N	H	O	A	W	M	E	B	L	Z	B	M	D
S	O	N	A	E	D	D	N	A	L	Y	A	W	S	O

CARL WARWICK
DAVE ROBERTSON
HOOKS WARNER
ALLEN ELLIOTT
OTTO VOGEL
TONY KAUFMANN
BUCK FREEMAN
OSCAR FUHR
WAYLAND DEAN
FRED FUSSELL
ELMER JACOBS
BILL PIERCY

They Had To Know Which Way the Wind Blew

```
L N O T G N I V O C S E W M D
V I N L R E D N O P R E M L E
O J D O C G E S S L E R A G S
K I G U G W M F R O A R L I U
R K L J S D E N E I E L H Y R
E S N A I P D A L G K H W O R
T W R C A M E M Z F G T A E A
L O A K Y I M T T A N S T R M
O K D S M T I Y E O L R H N T
W R N O R F E S M S A I C E I
Y O F N E L B S X C C D E S R
R B E I E U T R E S M O L N V
R B W E T J I O L I O A T I T
A O T R A N J I A N O P T T O
H B T R E K S A P E D O D H P
```

HOWIE FITZGERALD
DODE PASKERT
LOU JACKSON
PETE SCOTT
BOB BORKOWSKI
JOE CARTER
ALEX METZLER
DOC GESSLER
HARRY WOLTER
ELMER PONDER
WES COVINGTON
JIMMY MCMATH

Blink, And You Would Have Missed Them

Z	A	R	Y	M	C	I	L	L	A	N	A	S	J	H
T	E	R	E	C	S	I	H	R	O	T	C	I	V	N
L	B	E	N	T	N	E	A	H	C	I	M	L	O	A
A	R	J	R	K	H	A	B	E	K	W	M	D	S	O
N	E	H	U	N	V	C	W	I	O	L	I	G	R	M
N	Y	S	B	X	I	A	I	O	J	R	U	W	E	F
C	O	I	K	I	M	E	D	R	R	U	L	I	U	N
I	R	M	C	S	P	S	O	O	E	K	M	X	Q	P
S	C	Q	A	S	O	R	C	V	V	I	C	F	E	I
R	O	U	L	E	T	K	M	T	I	N	G	A	U	E
E	T	E	B	S	N	I	I	U	J	T	V	G	J	C
I	D	R	L	A	P	O	L	N	H	C	Z	E	E	O
V	O	T	R	Z	A	M	L	G	O	K	O	D	L	R
A	U	F	A	N	I	T	E	O	C	N	E	L	B	E
R	D	T	E	S	E	C	R	O	P	R	I	E	A	K

EARL BLACKBURN
FRANK CORRIDON
ERNIE OVITZ
REGGIE RICHTER
JIM WOODS
DOC MILLER
JACK ROWAN

Yessirree, Bob

A	B	O	B	O	F	A	R	R	E	L	L	T	L	E
N	O	O	S	T	R	E	H	P	N	A	S	N	W	V
E	B	E	B	E	N	T	R	Y	T	Y	A	O	X	I
O	K	M	Y	S	T	B	A	O	A	O	B	S	E	S
D	E	A	P	R	C	Y	E	U	N	O	T	R	D	F
L	L	O	E	T	U	A	H	R	B	D	J	E	W	E
E	L	F	S	P	Y	B	N	O	A	O	E	T	A	I
P	Y	L	D	R	S	O	S	L	U	S	T	T	Y	R
H	N	O	N	E	D	B	R	K	A	E	I	A	L	C
A	I	N	T	W	O	R	O	N	W	N	S	P	N	N
S	A	P	E	R	O	N	C	B	I	E	O	B	D	U
R	I	H	N	D	T	F	E	B	O	T	T	O	N	M
E	N	G	G	N	I	F	F	E	H	C	S	B	O	B
F	Y	G	O	F	E	T	E	T	O	P	N	K	O	O
R	O	M	T	I	A	R	S	N	E	R	D	I	C	B

BOB O'FARRELL
BOB SPEAKE
BOB SCHEFFING
BOB PATTERSON
BOB TEWKSBURY
BOB OSBORN
BOB KELLY
BOB MUNCRIEF
BOB SCANLAN

They Made Their Home In the Dirt

```
D Y R N O S L O T K C I H C M
L W T E R C E M F I S U E H A
E F O R L J L U S A L G A N H
I K R N A T S Y B B U R I N T
F I R A A I U O D T V T J I N
S T D E N G R B I E R C A M A
N A R K K K A O Y A B A S L R
A L S V A C G H M N L E O N G
R O N O R D E U O E N E C E E
B B U R L N T B S L G H P K G
Y A D O D S S B Z T A R O H R
T I K R L I E A J N I H O J O
T W I A H L M A L D I N S E E
I C E A L R E K E T B E E A G
K S P T R E B O L S N A H L E
```

FRANK GUSTINE
GEORGE MORIARTY
KITTY BRANSFIELD
GEORGE GRANTHAM
HARVEY HENDRICK
CHICK TOLSON
STU MARTIN

HAL O'HAGAN
ART BUES
HEINZ BECKER
LES BELL
CLYDE BECK
HANS LOBERT
JOHNNY BUTLER

Legends

S	S	H	T	I	S	K	N	A	B	E	I	N	R	E
X	M	M	A	N	F	R	T	H	N	D	L	Y	O	H
N	A	A	S	C	O	U	O	Y	T	H	N	R	K	T
R	I	R	O	S	K	S	R	N	I	E	I	G	C	I
U	L	K	S	E	T	W	W	O	S	E	R	E	O	F
B	L	G	Y	T	A	E	I	A	M	A	S	A	R	F
H	I	R	M	D	T	B	N	L	D	R	N	R	B	I
S	W	A	M	Y	A	D	A	O	S	E	T	T	U	R
A	Y	C	A	E	B	P	O	C	T	O	R	A	O	G
E	L	E	S	E	L	W	L	M	N	W	N	D	L	K
I	L	P	R	E	Y	U	A	P	O	S	G	N	N	R
H	I	G	A	R	O	I	G	H	T	N	W	I	T	A
C	B	F	R	I	M	S	R	Y	H	E	S	N	O	L
I	A	E	D	R	A	W	O	H	L	E	D	E	T	C
R	K	R	E	L	L	I	V	N	A	R	A	M	R	H

BILLY WILLIAMS
CLARK GRIFFITH
KERRY WOOD
DEL HOWARD
RAFAEL PALMEIRO
MARK GRACE
R. (RABBIT) MARANVILLE
ERNIE BANKS
ANDRE DAWSON
HACK WILSON
RYNE SANDBERG
SAMMY SOSA
LOU BROCK
RICHIE ASHBURN

Seems Like Only Yesterday When We Saw...

J	E	R	R	Y	M	U	M	P	H	R	E	Y	G	O
E	U	W	O	M	I	S	H	A	O	E	C	H	N	H
R	L	N	I	A	N	Y	A	U	M	E	D	A	I	E
R	D	H	I	K	E	N	T	L	V	O	S	K	L	T
Y	O	L	D	O	C	G	E	A	W	A	E	D	I	O
M	N	D	B	T	R	E	R	S	H	N	N	N	A	D
O	A	I	E	G	T	K	L	S	H	A	R	L	R	W
R	D	C	V	R	N	E	E	E	R	F	E	T	F	I
A	E	K	O	G	H	P	N	N	I	I	S	H	N	W
L	V	T	K	G	Y	D	E	M	N	B	H	C	E	D
E	I	I	K	H	E	L	M	A	A	E	E	O	K	E
S	L	D	T	R	E	P	O	C	O	N	D	K	C	J
A	W	R	S	O	A	R	S	H	E	P	N	Y	I	L
F	R	O	G	S	D	A	V	E	R	A	D	E	R	M
D	N	W	A	S	A	N	E	R	I	T	A	R	T	Y

GREG GROSS
LEN RANDLE
KEN HENDERSON
JUNIOR KENNEDY
PAUL ASSENMACHER
JERRY MUMPHREY

DICK TIDROW
KEN FRAILING
JERRY MORALES
MIKE BIELECKI
DAVE RADER
KEN KRAVEC

More Northside Names

O	F	R	T	D	L	E	F	N	I	E	T	S	H	O
L	S	T	U	C	K	S	T	A	I	N	B	A	C	K
K	T	A	U	S	A	Y	R	E	O	L	Y	A	N	O
I	R	A	T	S	S	U	R	B	N	E	R	R	A	W
L	J	L	E	S	D	M	S	N	F	U	R	C	L	J
A	I	K	O	R	I	W	E	S	B	U	E	A	L	I
W	M	E	C	U	E	D	A	E	D	O	T	N	I	M
O	M	B	L	A	S	T	C	Y	R	H	B	I	M	M
K	I	O	Y	Y	M	T	S	E	O	S	E	R	C	Y
N	E	S	K	D	O	O	R	B	L	N	Z	B	M	C
A	F	U	I	G	M	D	W	I	E	A	L	E	M	O
I	O	S	R	M	L	A	K	Y	N	W	T	L	R	O
B	X	N	E	O	V	Y	B	C	N	G	Y	I	O	N
A	X	R	O	S	M	E	A	U	A	O	E	A	N	E
F	S	F	U	N	K	I	T	O	M	J	T	R	R	Y

WARREN BRUSSTAR
TUCK STAINBACK
RAY WEBSTER
FABIAN KOWALIK
JIMMY COONEY
NORM MCMILLAN
RUSS MEERS
ALEC DISTASO
TONY WOMACK
LOU STRINGER
JACK DOYLE
ZEB TERRY
RUDY SOMMERS
JIMMIE FOXX

Names From the 90s

E	L	J	A	M	E	S	D	R	I	S	A	T	A	W
N	R	O	E	A	F	W	N	K	O	R	E	I	J	Z
O	A	S	D	F	I	E	A	Y	R	I	D	U	A	E
S	L	E	L	U	F	L	L	R	K	E	B	T	C	L
R	E	N	C	P	V	R	L	S	R	A	T	I	C	A
E	H	I	O	S	I	P	O	E	R	E	G	H	A	Z
K	I	E	T	E	L	B	H	B	L	A	A	W	R	N
C	G	V	I	R	N	X	L	L	I	D	C	S	D	O
I	T	E	B	W	I	M	U	O	M	N	T	H	I	G
N	E	S	A	L	N	B	M	E	G	B	S	U	E	I
N	P	H	E	O	T	U	Y	D	R	N	U	O	N	M
A	S	F	D	T	R	E	R	M	S	E	O	J	N	E
Y	P	A	O	L	R	O	R	E	H	M	T	U	O	R
R	N	C	D	S	K	R	E	T	R	O	P	O	B	E
B	S	O	T	C	O	Y	T	I	T	S	A	E	R	G

FELIX HEREDIA
GEREMI GONZALEZ
TERRY MULHOLLAND
BRYAN HICKERSON
SHAWN BOSKIE
BO PORTER
JOSE NIEVES
SCOTT BULLETT
CHAD MEYERS
JEFF ROBINSON

The Year Was 2006, the Pitchers Were…

```
R H C S U R N O D N E L G Y W
L E C D C M H A N U N O L I S
C Y T I N T I A H A X L X M N
I S G S K O M K L R I P A A A
R R C H P H R C E B U I J O N
D Y M O O M O L M W L D I V G
E R A L T G E R A L U K M O E
F A L N S T L D I W I E S N L
F I R F O G E W N E S F R O G
W G O N D M E Y E A P E K T U
T S W Y I M A J R O Y K L R Z
A I M L O B A L V E A R E E M
Z V L R O T E O L O Z B M B A
E E E U Y R K U K E A J A O N
R J T I M M E S A C Y P L R S
```

WADE MILLER
RYAN DEMPSTER
ANGEL GUZMAN
JEROME WILLIAMS
SCOTT EYRE
JAE KUK RYU

MIKE WUERTZ
RYAN O'MALLEY
WILL OHMAN
LES WALROND
GLENDON RUSCH
ROBERTO NOVOA

AB's Are Great – 1902 History Begins

```
N U E R S E N O J Y V A D D T
S E C S M A I L L I W O T T O
G F R A T E H O R U S H N I R
G S A E R S U M W O I D A E Y
I T L M M L A T H E B S K Y H
R O U S E I L I A O F N T E T
B U T S I L E U B V I A F L R
S M A I L L I W N T T O B D A
N R A L E E I C E D O F R G C
O Y E S A C C O D K G N O E C
T I M Y K M J O D H A R W O M
T S R E V E Y N N H O J E R K
U D R U H C A N K D A V E N C
B N O D I R R O C K N A R F A
S I R R A L L I E N O K C A J
```

JOHNNY EVERS	JOE TINKER
FRANK CORRIDON	DOC CASEY
JACK MCCARTHY	OTTO WILLIAMS
JACK O'NEILL	BOB WICKER
JAKE WEIMER	BUTTONS BRIGGS
CARL LUNDGREN	DAVY JONES

With a Little Lakeshore In Their Drive

F	Y	C	A	B	I	L	L	M	A	D	L	O	C	K
I	B	N	Y	R	O	M	T	L	A	W	O	R	T	E
R	L	A	M	A	R	K	N	U	E	Z	A	R	I	V
G	A	V	B	I	R	O	O	M	A	M	I	B	M	I
E	S	E	O	E	B	E	S	O	I	X	I	O	M	N
N	E	R	T	L	D	L	L	X	C	L	A	B	Y	T
S	P	R	C	E	L	A	O	L	L	S	M	R	K	S
T	I	N	O	A	E	E	H	Y	I	E	P	A	C	U
U	N	O	W	J	I	M	C	L	E	M	Y	H	A	E
K	A	E	E	K	T	O	I	R	G	R	K	I	H	G
O	E	L	N	Z	W	T	N	A	R	R	E	C	N	R
L	M	A	I	A	U	S	L	E	L	G	E	T	A	A
O	R	T	N	E	D	C	L	J	O	E	R	N	T	H
F	H	A	N	K	L	E	I	B	E	R	A	H	S	T
A	E	V	O	D	A	Z	B	I	C	O	T	S	E	W

HACK MILLER
BABE DAHLGREN
STAN HACK
LEE WALLS
BILL MADLOCK
HANK LEIBER
BILL NICHOLSON
WALT MORYN
BILLY COWAN

148

H	T	E	T	I	H	W	L	L	E	D	N	O	R	L
N	C	H	A	D	M	E	Y	E	R	S	E	J	I	O
O	O	I	Z	G	E	B	I	L	L	D	S	W	S	H
A	K	S	J	E	N	N	A	L	A	W	L	A	C	C
S	E	C	R	I	N	U	D	M	E	O	E	A	E	I
A	N	A	O	E	D	I	O	H	T	R	L	J	R	N
C	D	D	R	R	T	N	T	Y	S	M	O	R	T	C
H	E	E	C	A	B	T	N	R	C	A	I	N	Y	M
K	R	L	I	U	A	K	A	L	A	I	A	N	D	N
O	A	O	F	M	E	S	I	P	O	M	R	E	V	A
V	L	O	Y	B	T	S	O	R	Y	G	E	E	O	I
A	R	R	U	I	H	R	N	A	R	E	L	V	H	R
D	A	O	L	G	S	S	O	R	U	A	R	P	A	B
G	N	A	Z	E	T	I	N	O	R	D	T	O	R	D
Z	E	R	I	T	U	G	E	I	L	L	I	W	C	P

BRIAN MCNICHOL
CHAD MEYERS
TARRIK BROCK
ROSS GLOAD
GARY MATTHEWS, JR.
COREY PATTERSON
CAL MCLISH
ERIC YOUNG
DAMON BUFORD
DAVE MARTINEZ
RONDELL WHITE

149

H	G	U	O	L	L	O	C	C	M	E	D	Y	L	C
O	Y	O	R	L	E	C	M	K	C	U	H	C	A	L
N	J	C	H	I	T	A	S	A	R	D	Y	R	R	O
A	L	A	G	R	E	S	T	X	I	N	L	L	A	M
I	Y	O	C	L	I	F	F	F	L	O	Y	D	M	R
R	E	Y	M	Q	J	D	U	T	S	L	E	N	I	A
O	O	V	R	R	U	O	K	Z	W	R	M	O	S	M
S	N	A	R	W	A	E	A	R	R	T	L	E	R	S
O	I	T	E	I	O	M	J	E	A	P	S	S	A	O
S	C	S	K	S	B	H	K	O	H	E	M	T	M	L
N	V	A	W	R	M	L	B	M	N	I	I	H	I	R
O	R	K	A	O	E	N	E	O	A	E	J	A	R	A
F	O	N	R	E	D	N	O	W	B	D	S	N	E	C
L	O	N	E	D	E	C	Y	N	N	O	R	R	Z	E
A	L	L	A	D	N	E	K	N	O	S	A	J	A	Y

CARLOS ZAMBRANO
JASON KENDALL
DERREK LEE
JACQUE JONES
CARLOS MARMOL
CLYDE MCCULLOUGH
CHUCK MCELROY
CLIFF FLOYD
ARAMIS RAMIREZ
RONNY CEDENO
BOB HOWRY
ALFONSO SORIANO

150

```
M F I B W R E H C O L L O H C
D E R I T S U I G E V A D T O
N A R A Y K I N G C N H R R K
O L R I N I B U P A E E R R N
R J I O T K A L M G G A E V E
L D U O L S D Z L N Z O P S R
A E T A R D U I I I N S R H E
W N I A N G K L P U H I E O V
S N M R L M M N G I R H T W E
E I A E A E A M O E N V C U T
L S G I R U A T D W V O M I S
O N E E J D L I E K L A E N R
A S K M O Q U E S O L E D T I
D I R T N A V E R N O L S E N
M S A S S O F Y N O T S I R B
```

MIKE REMLINGER	DAVE GIUSTI
ANGEL GUZMAN	RAY KING
DAROLD KNOWLES	RICH HILL
JUAN PIZARRO	FRANK DIPINO
JUAN MATEO	LES WALROND
STEVE RENKO	VERN OLSEN
C. (CHARLIE) HOLLOCHER	TONY FOSSAS

151

M	C	H	R	W	R	E	G	A	K	U	I	N	L	T
E	I	C	G	A	R	Y	V	A	R	S	H	O	E	O
R	D	K	S	R	Z	T	I	N	E	T	E	K	P	G
I	L	M	E	G	S	A	R	O	A	L	B	E	A	F
T	A	J	U	H	R	A	L	N	T	L	U	K	C	D
N	L	O	E	R	A	E	O	A	A	B	R	I	E	W
I	N	E	C	F	D	R	B	N	S	E	C	M	K	A
C	I	J	K	I	W	N	K	D	I	L	T	L	I	L
M	P	E	R	K	P	E	A	E	N	A	E	L	M	E
Y	P	C	C	P	N	F	M	L	Y	U	W	G	I	C
R	E	I	V	S	N	E	F	T	L	W	S	A	N	N
R	R	V	H	E	V	I	L	E	N	L	Y	M	A	A
A	A	I	R	A	A	D	O	O	J	M	I	T	I	V
H	P	Y	D	E	N	R	E	T	S	G	U	B	A	J
I	D	L	A	R	I	H	C	S	N	I	V	L	A	C

K. (KEVIN) BLANKENSHIP
MIKE HARKEY
AL NIPPER
CALVIN SCHIRALDI
RICK WRONA
ANGEL SALAZAR
HARRY MCINTIRE
MIKE CAPEL
BILL LANDRUM
JEFF PICO
JIM SUNDBERG
DAVE MEIER
GARY VARSHO
VANCE LAW

151 Almost There

S	P	A	N	I	T	O	X	O	C	A	L	Y	B	R
T	T	E	L	L	U	B	T	T	O	C	S	L	O	W
J	A	J	P	R	I	L	T	E	N	H	N	S	P	H
G	E	I	E	V	T	K	C	R	A	E	S	W	E	A
N	O	F	V	F	W	O	L	W	S	T	E	O	S	N
I	M	R	F	O	F	D	N	N	G	I	G	R	E	E
N	U	B	A	R	T	B	A	O	B	S	E	A	I	N
D	N	A	L	L	O	H	L	U	M	Y	R	R	E	T
O	N	U	H	S	E	B	L	A	E	X	O	L	O	D
R	E	D	K	V	C	L	I	M	U	N	L	A	S	M
A	Y	I	A	L	E	O	D	N	I	S	C	G	H	U
L	E	D	M	T	F	A	T	V	S	O	E	S	I	Y
D	E	P	T	E	H	I	E	T	N	O	C	R	K	B
O	H	O	S	C	A	K	O	B	E	R	N	D	P	O
Y	T	S	O	I	L	G	I	V	E	R	D	W	A	L

TERRY MULHOLLAND
DAVE HANSEN
SHAWN BOSKIE
JEFF BLAUSER
SCOTT BULLETT
JEFF ROBINSON
CHAD MEYERS
KEVIN ORIE

1906 – 1st Place Team Members

T	N	O	M	U	A	E	B	R	E	G	N	I	G	J
O	D	E	T	I	N	K	E	N	A	L	D	W	I	E
H	R	L	O	G	A	I	E	T	D	C	A	M	I	G
E	A	V	E	R	Y	R	L	E	T	L	M	H	E	K
L	E	R	A	F	M	C	L	O	Y	Y	C	W	P	N
O	H	Y	R	L	N	H	U	F	S	I	U	A	R	O
C	S	F	O	Y	O	I	E	H	R	D	T	G	O	V
G	A	L	T	W	M	V	E	W	C	M	D	O	L	E
N	N	O	A	U	N	C	E	T	O	W	H	D	Y	N
I	D	R	L	O	K	L	I	R	S	I	E	B	A	B
K	D	T	S	A	I	R	A	N	A	Y	B	Y	T	E
R	O	B	R	C	S	N	I	N	T	L	R	U	K	T
N	E	D	R	D	E	N	W	W	S	I	L	R	C	C
I	C	H	I	C	K	F	R	A	S	E	R	Y	A	O
W	O	L	A	S	E	W	R	I	C	H	I	E	Z	H

HARRY STEINFELDT
CHICK FRASER
GINGER BEAUMONT
HARRY MCINTIRE
JIMMY SHECKARD
ORVAL OVERALL
ZACK TAYLOR
DEL HOWARD
KING COLE
LEW RICHIE
PAT MORAN

The End

R	A	Z	I	C	O	N	F	U	Y	S	N	E	N	D
C	S	U	L	F	I	E	T	R	E	A	B	G	A	D
B	N	W	H	A	T	R	N	D	G	M	O	R	M	L
M	I	O	E	A	T	E	A	E	I	C	O	D	Y	L
E	Y	L	T	A	H	E	R	L	K	L	I	S	R	E
O	M	E	L	L	G	L	C	A	D	C	O	E	F	N
H	E	T	L	S	I	O	B	K	K	E	R	L	E	S
L	B	I	T	H	T	M	N	R	O	R	S	O	I	S
P	B	W	P	P	F	O	A	M	U	A	M	N	D	E
U	T	E	G	K	W	D	N	H	A	H	O	E	O	R
C	O	N	O	L	A	O	I	E	E	R	X	V	O	P
A	M	K	E	T	H	D	P	C	M	V	K	I	W	T
L	S	S	Z	S	A	G	R	O	M	A	E	N	S	O
L	L	E	N	S	E	R	P	T	O	T	N	T	E	T
R	E	V	E	T	S	W	I	N	D	Y	W	E	S	O

BILL HENRY
TOT PRESSNELL
DAROLD KNOWLES
BILL STONEMAN
WOODIE FRYMAN
STEVE HAMILTON
DICK RADATZ
PHIL REGAN

MY IMAGINARY EX

CHIC MANILA #1

MINA V. ESGUERRA

BRIGHT GIRL BOOKS

This book is a work of fiction. Names, characters, places, and incidents are products of the author's imagination or are used fictitiously. Any resemblance to actual events or locales or persons, living or dead, is entirely coincidental.

Cover designed by Tania Arpa

Photography by Alexandra Urrea

Publication history

First published in 2009 by Summit Books

A revised edition appeared in the *Perfect Boyfriends* compilation, published in 2014 by Bright Girl Books

This expanded edition published in 2017 by Bright Girl Books

That this book even happened is due to the following people, whether they know it or not:

Louie, who patiently edited a novel I wrote, except it wasn't this one. But the comments she gave helped shape everything I wrote after.

Iggy, who wrote her stories, got published, and told me how to get it done.

Mimi, who kind of made it all so.

Ines, for expertly guiding me through the genre.

My grandmothers, Lola Zoring and Lola Pris, for the support and encouragement.

My family, for bearing with my noisy typewriter in the early '90s.

And Mike, who is awesome, always.

ONE

Lena was one of those friends who never called.

That in itself wasn't unusual. Five years since college graduation; people moved on. I was only in touch with a handful of people, most of them from my AB Psychology block. Lena was not from that block. We weren't even in the same orgs or the same barkada.

I tried to recall how we were friends. For some reason her name triggered stress and anxiety in me, but I couldn't figure out why. And then: *Oh, right.*

Zack. She was the ex of my friend Zack.

Then I remembered why my stomach was doing little nervous flips. Lena Mallari was the recipient of one of the longest-running lies I had ever told, and after almost ten years, I could no longer keep my stories straight. So I decided to avoid her as much as possible.

Out of the blue, I got a text from her: *Jas, Coffee Bean, 6 tonight. BE THERE. Even if you have other plans, stop by. Need to talk to you, urgent.*

In my first year of college, I told Lena that Zachary Tomas—the cute guy who asked her to the Freshman Night party—was my high school boyfriend. It was not true, but I never came clean about it.

While walking to the coffee shop, I tried to piece together every single detail woven into that story. I couldn't remember it all. Maybe this was the day to admit it? After all, she and Zack had been broken up for years.

"Jasmine! I thought you weren't going to show up." Lena smiled widely. "Chai latte?"

"Sure."

I watched Lena lean a cylindrical object (yoga mat?) against our table as she stood up and headed to the counter. She was slender and perky, with a head full of lush curly hair. I remember she had a health kick in college, and wasn't surprised she did yoga.

She returned with a tea latte a size larger than what I was used to. Like she was expecting this "meeting" of ours to last longer than I thought. I got nervous.

"You look great!" she gushed, as if we were close friends. "Did you do something different to your hair? It looks so nice."

Oh, you mean actually brushing it? I had a tomboyish ponytail going on in college. Now I actually made an effort to style my hair, which I had grown past my shoulders. The whole production took half an hour each morning, but at least the waves in my hair looked like I *wanted* them there.

It was nice that she noticed. "Thanks, Lena. It's like you haven't changed at all."

She seemed to take it as a compliment, and it was. "So, how are you? Where are you working again?"

"I'm good. I'm in HR for a BPO."

"Do you work the night shift?"

"Sometimes. But not usually."

"Were you always there? I thought you worked at a pharma company after college."

"I moved. Been at this office for three years now." I sipped my tea, trying to ignore the awkwardness. "And you?"

"I've actually quit my job! Trying to get my own business running."

Lena started to tell me about the business she started, something to do with designing accessories, and that she had opened a small store. I asked her a few follow-up questions, to keep her talking about herself, consequently putting less pressure on me to share.

I'd always been introverted, but I got better at talking to people. I discovered that the key was to ask questions. Keep them talking for a while, and you'll hardly need to do anything.

Lena was in mid-sentence when she checked her watch, a frustrated look on her face. "I can't believe this. I said *six o'clock*."

"Why, Lena? What's up?"

"Jas, I guess I should just start. Do you have a boyfriend?"

"What? Well, no."

"Good. That's good."

I started to panic. "Wait! Are you setting me up with somebody?"

"No, no. Or maybe. Have you talked to Zack lately?"

Uh-oh! "No," I said, and that was the truth. "I think the last time I heard from him was... it's got to be months."

"You got an invitation to his wedding, right?"

"Yes." This conversation was becoming even weirder. "Did you?"

"No. We didn't stay friends after college. Do you know anything about his fiancée, Kimmy?"

"I've met her, but I don't really know her."

Lena sighed. "This is going to be harder than I thought then. Jasmine, I was going to ask you to stage some sort of intervention for our Zack."

"What?"

"I want you to get him to break his engagement. Call off the wedding. Do anything, just keep him from marrying that girl."

TWO

College, nine years ago

NOT MANY OF my high school classmates were in my university. I knew a few people, recognized another dozen faces, but none of my friends were there.

Zack was one of those familiar faces who wasn't really a friend. We were in line for spaghetti carbonara in the cafeteria on the first week of school, and he talked to me first.

"Are you the girl who sang with the little kids at last year's Environment Day?" he asked, unexpectedly.

"Yes," I replied, cringing. "Please, not so loud."

"I thought I recognized you from high school! You were great."

"Do you see me hanging out with people from our school? No."

"Your secret is safe with me," he grinned. "I'm Zack Tomas."

"Jasmine Salazar."

We took our plates of over-sauced pasta and he followed

me to an unoccupied table. I hesitated, the instinct to shun people from high school kicking in. It was hard, moving to a new school and not having any of my friends, but I consoled myself by deciding to start fresh. To reinvent myself. It could also be because I was naturally shy (yes, despite the singing—singing to a crowd is easier than talking to a stranger), and found making new friends a challenge.

This reinvention was *not* going to work if I had Zack (who might remember embarrassing things about me) hanging around. However?

Zack was cute. I figured he wasn't tall enough for basketball varsity, but he was still a few inches taller than me. That day at the cafeteria, his hair was shaved close to his head but was just starting to grow again. He said his hair wasn't normally like that and that he regretted the cut. I had since seen him with probably two other hairstyles and I had to agree.

He *did* look better with his dark brown hair a little longer. When we met, he looked like he was dressed for a game with the guys—shorts, basketball shoes, white shirt. He looked solid and athletic, not exactly typical of the geek he later proclaimed to be.

Better him than anyone else from the other sort-of familiar faces.

Then I remembered what *he* did in high school—he was on the basketball team in our senior year. I think he had a remarkable game against the very tall sophomores. For a while, people were talking about him being a "lucky find." Our batch had never won a basketball game, and we ended up taking home the championship in our final year.

"Yeah, my fifteen minutes of fame." Humbly, or dismissively, Zack shrugged it off. "That went by too quickly. I didn't think I'd be good at it."

"What were you doing all those years when we were losing? To *freshmen?*"

"I didn't think I was good enough," he admitted. "When we were seniors, someone sprained an ankle and they pushed me in at the last minute."

"Well, I had a *great* time at that game," I said. "Those sophomores were too arrogant. It was nice to see them bite it."

"Glad I helped you with that."

I learned most of what I knew about Zack in college. Even though we named every single member of our respective barkadas, we didn't have any common friends.

We had a nice lunch. Not the best meal, but we both remembered that day. Right before we graduated, we had a last lunch at the cafeteria, recreating that moment. He snapped a photo of me with a forkful of pasta in my mouth to save on his phone.

That photo showed up on his screen whenever I texted or called, years after it was taken. Even when he lost his phone, he reloaded the same pic into the replacement, and even when he became a management trainee at a big consumer goods company, that pic still showed up whenever I rang.

Zack was in a Management course, and I was in Psychology, so we hung out with other people.

He would drop by my usual tambayan, asking if I felt like a burger/coffee/loaning him money for photocopying, but he wouldn't hang out.

"Who's that?" my friends would ask each time he came by.

Something we discovered we had in common was that neither of us felt like joining a tight-knit barkada right away. He wanted to remain a "free agent" because he thought that his friends from high school (somewhat geeky smart boys) held him back from exploring his less geeky interests (basketball).

I was just not comfortable with a huge clique.

I preferred a few close friends that I really liked hanging out with. That gelled well with Zack's own quirk of keeping his friends separate.

Like, he never ate lunch with the guys he played basketball with. Or he never studied with his friends from his org.

I asked him why he did that.

He looked at me like *duh.* "So no single person knows everything about me."

I rolled my eyes. "You have intimacy issues."

Those intimacy issues were put to the test when my friend Zack met Lena Mallari in Zoology class, second semester. I wouldn't have known if he didn't say anything, since I never saw him if he didn't seek me out. Apparently, they had started having lunch together.

The first time I met Lena was when she approached me while I was in line at the copy machine.

"Are you Jasmine Salazar?" she asked.

Being taller, awkward, and having to look down at her self-assured, tiny frame did not make things easy for me. I had grown three inches in a few years and didn't know what to do with my arms. I seemed to be forever outgrowing a bad haircut, so the default hairdo was a ponytail. She was petite, and at that time, the only girl I had seen with wild Keri Russell hair who wasn't straightening it in any way.

But what stood out for me was how she was so naturally friendly.

"Yes," I said, unsure of what was happening. "I'm sorry, are we classmates?"

"No, no. Sorry. I'm Lena. I was... I saw you and I'm not

sure if this is proper but what the hell, I'm here anyway. Zack Tomas asked me to Freshman Night this Friday. Are you okay with that?"

Freshman Night was a party that was going to be in one of the campus dorms. It was an annual thing, usually early into the second semester. I didn't think it was formal and required dates, but I guessed that was what people did in college.

But what confused me was why she sounded like she was asking my permission. "Of course I'm okay with it."

She let out a breath, so relieved that she actually hopped a little. "Cool! Thanks. I know you two still hang out together, so I wanted to check if you were fine with it. He didn't tell you that he asked me?"

I still wasn't sure what she was talking about, and by now I was *very* aware that the five other people in line *plus* the copy girl were listening to us.

"No he didn't, Lena, but he doesn't have to tell me if he asks anyone out."

"That's nice. I was just making sure. Thanks, Jasmine."

She pretty much skipped away, and I was left in line, blushing, trying to pretend that didn't just happen.

That day, Zack left a message at my tambayan and on my locker. Two identical messages in two different places, informing me that he needed to talk to me. He finally caught up with me as I got out of my last class.

I went first. "I met Lena today. Why is she asking me for permission to go out with you?"

"Huh?" He looked taken aback. "Why would she do that?"

"I don't know! It was very weird."

"What did you tell her?"

"What do you mean? Of course I said she can go out with you!"

He looked sheepish. "Yeah so that's why I needed to talk to you. She thinks you're my ex-girlfriend from high school."

"What? Why would she think that?"

"I was going to warn you first but I didn't know she'd be so...well she's got initiative, I guess."

"Sorry but why is this even a thing? Am I supposed to *do* anything?"

Zack, it turned out, did not have a girlfriend in high school. He had never had a girlfriend, and Lena was the first girl he had asked out, ever.

"*Ever*?" I didn't believe it. Even *I* was asked out once or twice before. And I wasn't even on a sports team. "What about senior prom?"

"I didn't go with a date," he said. "The girl I was interested in wasn't...anyway, I went with my friends."

I started laughing. "I feel bad for you and your friends."

"Prom's overrated. It's more fun with friends."

"Of course you would say that. Hard to explain it now that you're trying to impress a girl?"

His problem was that in getting to know Lena, he learned that she did not want to go out with guys who had never had prior relationships.

"I don't want to waste my time," was how she described it. "I don't want to be the guinea pig, you know? Like, first girlfriends always get the mistakes. They fix their guys up, and then the next girlfriend benefits! It's not fair."

Lena was a practical one, I had to admit. "I'm guessing she's been the first girlfriend at least once before."

"So how could I tell her that I'm new at this, right? She'll reject me even before she gets to know me."

"Well she didn't reject you. She told me she's going with you to Freshman Night. Congratulations, I guess."

It could have ended there. Lena asked, I answered, they were going on a date.

But Zack had an idea.

"Jas, I need a favor. She already thinks you're my ex anyway."

"Oh no...what do you want?"

"Can you...I don't know, can you tell her nice things about me? We can hang out together on Freshman Night, and when you get her alone, you can drop hints like I'm into her or something. I'm awesome. I'd be a great boyfriend."

"You want me to lie."

"It won't be a lie!"

"You've never been a great boyfriend! You've never *been* a boyfriend."

"Jas, you know our school, where we came from. You know the bad crowd. You know I'm not part of that."

"Yeah but you're asking me to *lie*."

"*Favor*."

We stared at each other, each no doubt composing the next retort, and I tried to remember him from high school. I knew he was there, in the background, but you know when your life revolved around a small group of people and everyone else was just scenery? That wasn't so bad—if he had been the wrong kind of person, I would have remembered him for the wrong things. That was how our school was. No drama was better than too much.

Looking back, it was probably the lamest favor ever asked of me, but at the time it sounded fun. And I knew where he came from. That mattered, when it was a place like college and everyone was a stranger.

He was probably needing the same anchor of sorts. He just didn't think of it that way.

"Sure," I said, helpful in a misguided way. "But can we do this my way? I can't go up to her at some party and tell her you like her. I can't be your ex and say you're great because that's fishy. We have to be more subtle. Also, you can't keep looking like you just rolled out of bed. Have some respect for the girl."

"What are you talking about?"

"That." I pointed to his unwashed jeans, wrinkled shirt (the same one from two days ago) and slippers. It was a little too slacker college boy. You'd expect that from a dormer who really *did* just roll out of bed. But Zack actually traveled an hour to get to school.

"Fine! Whatever you think will work." He looked happy and excited, and I felt a little pleased with my new role as his partner in crime.

IN THE WEEKS THAT FOLLOWED, Lena and I struck up an uneasy friendship. She was always the first to smile at me, say hello in the halls, or ask me to breakfast if she was heading to the cafeteria. I was sure it wasn't because of my dazzling personality—she probably wanted to keep the "enemy" close.

That was fine, because it allowed me to sing Zack's praises in ways that weren't obvious. I didn't need to drop heavy hints, Lena usually asked the questions first.

"So is Zack really different now?" she asked me one time, while we waited for our rides at the carpool terminal. "From high school, I mean."

"Yes and no."

"Huh?"

"He's much more confident now I think. It helps that he's with people who have similar interests." Not knowing much about who Zack was in high school, I started taking liberties with our recent history. "I think his high school friends held him back a little."

"Really?" This bit of personal insight made Lena's eyes light up. "How?"

"I mean, I never really knew what he wanted to do back then. He'd do things as an afterthought, like joining the basketball team in his last year."

"Wow. I didn't know he played basketball. Is he good?"

"Yes. Like, MVP if he had played longer."

"He was your first boyfriend?"

I guessed what she really wanted to know was if *I* was his first girlfriend. I didn't know what he had told her exactly. Did he have one girlfriend in high school or more? I shook my head and leaped into the lie.

"Yeah, it was first love and all that. It's corny."

"Of course not! High school love is so cute."

"I guess." I pretended to think it over. "I never really thought of him that way, you know? He told me that in grade two, he made this heart-shaped Valentine card for me, and he said I stuck it in my bag and pretended I never got it. It's weird because I don't remember that. But then in... in second year, I suddenly noticed him."

"Wow. Grade two? And he didn't give up on his childhood crush."

Okay, tone down the True Love, I told myself. A too-good story might scare her off. "Well, it wasn't that hard, because he was a chubby, klutzy kid. The girls didn't exactly fall over for him."

"Oh, I'd love to see pictures!"

Remind Zack NEVER to show Lena childhood pictures.

"Why did you break up?" Lena asked.

"Did he say anything about it?"

"No... I haven't really talked to him about anything this personal."

Good. "I... I went to the prom with someone else."

"What! You were still together?"

"Not exactly? I thought he wanted to break up after high school, so I said let's start now and go to the prom with other people. But then he didn't show up with a date, and I went with one of our friends. We never really recovered from that."

At the time, I was proud of myself for coming up with that story. It was plausible enough, and I mixed in real facts about the prom so if Lena actually talked to his real friends, they could confirm parts of it.

What wasn't good about that was that I eventually started to forget which parts I had made up. The truth was easy, but the versions of lies? The drafts of lies I didn't use, and what I ended up using? Woohoo.

But the important thing was that this particular story clinched it for Lena. She lapped it up, and I think it painted a picture of me as the villain in the relationship, and Zack as the kind, gentle, wounded party.

"But you're okay now? With each other? You seem to be friends again," she asked.

"Oh, we're okay now. Mostly because he's been such a gentleman about it. I told him at grad that we were going to the same school, and asked if he was okay with it. He hugged me and said he forgave me and that he'd like to remain friends."

And *that* painted Zack as some sort of hero boyfriend,

who graciously stayed friends with the ex who dumped him. How mature!

When I next saw him, I had to warn him about the things I told Lena. It didn't matter what he did with the information, as long as he didn't contradict it.

Lena became his girlfriend two weeks later.

THREE

Coffee shop, present day

MY MOUTH probably hung open for twenty seconds.

"Lena..." I said, wondering if she was kidding. "You're being silly."

No, she was not. She leaned forward, elbows on the table, looking very determined. "Absolutely not, Jas. You mean you don't know anything about Zack and Kimmy? Their relationship?"

Our friendship had stopped becoming a daily thing since college, especially when I got a boyfriend. We stayed in touch though, but we probably weren't as close as I thought. I found out about Kimmy the girlfriend *after* they had gotten together. Because he only really needed help that one time, and since then apparently had no trouble getting his own dates.

No need for sharing intimate details of anything. No need for new lies.

So I had gone from college partner-in-crime to sometime friend. He was there for me when I broke up with my boyfriend, but we didn't hang out regularly anymore. I wondered if he and his manager friends were too cool for me, but I never asked.

Such was our friendship. It never really lived up to its drama potential because we never exactly confronted each other about things.

"Kimmy is absolutely wrong for him," Lena declared. "And he's miserable, but he won't admit it."

"How do you know this?" I demanded. It annoyed me that she was telling me something about Zack's relationship that I didn't know. *Lena!* Of all people.

Lena lowered her voice and looked around furtively, remembering that we all worked in the same general area of Makati. "Well, I don't really have first-hand knowledge, but I have good sources. Why don't you know anything about this? A bunch of our college friends saw him in person recently, and they got to talk to him a little. Didn't he deliver your invite personally, like everyone else's?"

While Lena was essentially the same since college, I was different. In nine years, I had discovered how to move with some grace. I had joined the college choir. I had managed organizations and built up my confidence in dealing with people. But suddenly, it was like we were in line at the copier in school again.

"My invite was sent through the mail," I said. "I'm not sure what happened. I think we had a falling out."

Well, I wasn't completely sure until I got the invite, and yeah, that was it. At least I was invited, right? Like some college friend you never saw anymore. Like the past few years didn't—

What was it though?

What did I expect? I wasn't entitled to anything.

They probably didn't even really want me there. I took note of the RSVP info and the registry.

Like I'd even give them a gift.

"Well, that doesn't work." Lena shook her head, leaning back against her chair. "You can't cancel his wedding if you're not even on speaking terms."

"Why should I even do this? It's his choice if he wants to suffer. People marry people who are wrong for them *all the time*."

Yes, that was bitterness. I didn't know that he met up with college friends, while *I* got the invite sent so impersonally.

Lena didn't buy it. "Jas, you don't mean that. This is *Zack* we're talking about. Can you set aside whatever issues you have and think of what's best for him? I've been told that Kimmy is a manipulative, lying cheater, and always has been."

"Then why does he want to marry her?"

"I don't know, Jasmine. You studied psychology. Why does he keep having relationships with girls he isn't actually compatible with?"

"What do *you* think, Lena?"

She smiled slyly. She looked like she had been waiting to say this the entire evening. "Because he's never gotten over you, and he will deliberately get into doomed relationships until you finally realize you love him too and save him from himself."

I groaned. "I can't believe you're starting this again."

I wanted to say that she was wrong, that she couldn't *be more wrong*. Zack and I, I had to remind myself sometimes, were never together. There was nothing to "get over." There was no dramatic senior prom, no tearful "let's be friends" reconciliation during high school graduation. And if he really was in a doomed relationship then—his fault. I had nothing to do with it.

She was mistaken then, and mistaken now.

FOUR

College, seven years ago

"YOU SOUNDED GREAT," Zack said half-heartedly, handing me my school bag and jacket.

"I'm surprised you heard us at all. You look terrible."

Zack had offered to drive me home after choir practice, and was sitting by himself in the middle of the auditorium's third row the whole time. By my junior year, I had joined the choir.

Singing is the worst talent for a shy girl to have. Really. I discovered I could carry a tune in the shower, but it took years for me to get the nerve to perform for my family. The World Environment Day thing in high school was the only time I agreed to sing in school. I figured, what the hell, it was senior year anyway. If I was horrible, I only had a year to endure the teasing.

But I wasn't horrible, and Zack convinced me to try out for the college choir.

We were practicing for a Christmas performance, and I

could see him from my spot on stage. He looked miserable, sitting there staring into space.

As we walked to his car, he gave me the summary: he and Lena were having problems, and she brought up the idea that maybe they should break up.

"But you've been together for two years," I said. "What new problems could you possibly have?"

"They're old ones, actually."

"Well you *did* start your relationship with her with a lie." I was trying to make a joke when I said that by the way. "Aren't you ever going to tell her that I'm not your ex?"

He did not laugh at my joke. "The problems are all about the truth. And I'm never telling her about us."

"But it's hard having to remember what I told her. I don't even remember most of it myself. How do you do it?"

This, he laughed at. "I say, I'm not one to dwell on the past."

"So you haven't added anything new to the canon?" Zack was a bit of a comic book and fan fiction geek. "Canon" was *his* term, which he suddenly used to describe the collection of details about our fake relationship.

"No. I haven't told as many stories as you have, Jas. Most of the canon came from you."

"Great. I did all the work and you just reaped the rewards."

"You are a true friend."

He lived ten minutes away from my house. I watched him miss his own highway exit, in favor of the next one, which would lead us to my village first.

"So, how do we fix this problem with Lena?"

"What do you mean 'we'?" he asked. "This is my problem."

"Well, I'm your friend, right? And I'm a girl. Maybe there's a way I can reach out to Lena that you can't."

Zack adamantly refused any help. I couldn't imagine what his problem with Lena could be; he never complained about her. Never mentioned fighting with her. I'd sometimes see him in a bad mood, which usually meant he was thinking something through. But he never said anything bad about her.

He's really mature and thoughtful that way. I thought. *He DID forgive me for dumping him at prom—wait, that didn't actually happen.*

Sometimes I forgot too.

"PROBLEM? Did Zack talk to *you* about our 'problem'?"

Perhaps I had caught Lena at a bad time. She wasn't as relaxed as she usually was. She didn't look like she was in a hurry to go somewhere, but she sure looked annoyed at *me*.

"No," I said, quickly trying to save myself. "But he's been moody lately. He thinks something's wrong with the two of you, but he didn't say what. He wants to fix it though."

Lena petulantly hugged her binder, and I didn't need to be a psych major to know that she had just put up a wall between us. "Whatever the 'problem' is, it's none of your business, Jasmine. I am *done* with the two of you, honestly. I should lock you two in a room and you can either fight it out or end up together. Either way, I'm done."

"Wait! Lena, you don't mean that. It's not what you think—"

"It doesn't matter what you say, Jasmine. It's how it is."

"No, please, don't break up with him over this. Please,

think about it—maybe you misunderstood? We don't have feelings for each other. You might be seeing something completely innocent and giving it the wrong interpretation."

Lena paused at this, and her tight grip on her binder loosened a little. "Why does he tell you *everything*?"

"He doesn't."

"Well, fine, but why does he tell *you* everything he tells me? Shouldn't I come first?"

"You do, Lena. I don't even know where he is half the time. We don't even hang out."

Technically that was true. We spent most of our friendship in transit. On his way to the coffee shop? The library? The Math department? Drive me home from choir practice?

He'd wander over to my usual spots, and if I had nothing to do, I went along.

"I'm not friends with any of my exes. It's not healthy." She looked at me accusingly.

We share a secret, and that can really bind people together. I did not say that.

"Lena, it's not what you think. We're just friends, really."

"I don't treat my friends the way he treats you."

"Lena, you *liked* how mature he was when he forgave me and decided we should remain friends," I reminded her desperately.

That seemed to work. If Lena's defiance were a balloon, it started to deflate.

"Jasmine," she said. "Thanks for standing up for him, but this still is none of your business."

SHE BROKE up with him right before Christmas, but it looked like she stuck around and kept trying for three weeks after we talked.

I didn't tell Zack that Lena and I talked. From the looks of it, neither did Lena. So now that was a secret Lena and I shared. I probably had to write it all down at some point.

The news got to me on the last day of school, before the Christmas break. I was looking for Zack in his usual spot, and only saw Ramon, his block mate. I didn't know many of Zack's friends, but the year before, Ramon was my ballroom dancing partner in PE.

"Did he leave already?" I asked.

"Yeah," he replied. "Went home. Lena finally broke up with him."

"Just now?"

"They were talking by that tree for almost an hour."

I showed up at Zack's house with a half gallon of Double Dutch ice cream. The sight of me and my gift made him laugh. "I'm not a girl," he said.

"Trust me, this will make you feel better."

Zack, at first, didn't want to talk about Lena. I played the supportive friend and didn't ask, so instead he told me about his economics teacher, the electives he was thinking of taking, and the business idea he wanted to use as his thesis the following year. There was also a movie he wanted to watch that weekend, maybe I wanted to see it with him?

Two hours later, I couldn't wait anymore.

"Zack, about Lena..."

"I thought you wanted me to feel better."

"Talking will help resolve your issues."

"If you want to help, come with me to this movie. Robots at war! I'll feel better after that, I know it."

"Are you sure your problems weren't caused by our fake

relationship?" I asked. The way Lena reacted during our talk made me feel she was mad at me too, for some reason. It wasn't fair—I wasn't doing anything!

"I'm sure," he said, vehemently. Was he trying to protect me? He knew I'd feel bad if I had a role in their breakup, but he didn't know that Lena had spilled the beans, and some of those beans had my name on them.

"Well then. I think that next time, you shouldn't even bring it up. I think Lena's...impression of you was tainted by a lie. Next time, just be yourself."

Zack exhaled dramatically. "I didn't exactly think that one through, did I?"

"No." I scooped out another cup of ice cream for myself, finally accepting that we both kind of ruined that relationship together. I needed chocolate.

I reached over and squeezed his hand. "I'm sorry about Lena. You should never again tell anyone I was your girlfriend."

"That's a good idea."

FIVE

Coffee shop, present day

"ZACK DIDN'T ASK anyone out for *months* after you broke up with him," I said, offering that up as evidence of his true feelings for her. "You really messed him up."

Lena shook her head. "He didn't ask anyone out because you were there. He didn't *need* anyone else. I'm surprised you're still in denial about this." But she wasn't angry that I didn't believe her. If anything, she was amused.

After that awkward conversation in college, I did speak to Lena again. We were classmates in philosophy, and we eventually started saying quick hellos in the halls. At graduation, we even hugged—but I figured everyone was emotional that night.

"Are we really going to keep talking about this?" I whined.

"She's here! Finally." Lena's eyes darted to someone behind me, and I turned to look.

I almost choked on my tea. "Marjorie."

Marjorie Pineda had shorter hair now, and she'd lost some weight, looked more athletic. She took the empty seat next to me, and dropped the heavy bag she was carrying under the table.

Marjorie was Zack's second girlfriend.

"I'm sorry, I'm sorry, the meeting took longer than it should have," she said. "What have you talked about already?"

"I gave her the gist of what we want her to do," Lena said.

"Oh, of course." Marjorie turned to me, her eyes a little brighter. "And what did she say?"

"*She* is not on speaking terms with Zack."

"You're kidding me," Marjorie said, addressing me directly now. "What happened?"

I still wasn't sure what was happening but I answered her anyway. "I don't know. He just stopped—You know what? I don't have to explain anything to you. Or to you. How did you two even meet?"

"Yoga," Marjorie answered. "Didn't figure out who she was until I found out her last name."

When Marjorie saw Lena's name on the attendance list of her weekly yoga class, she immediately yelled, "As in the ex of Zack Tomas?!" in her typical borderline-tactless fashion. Apparently, she had never met Lena—she had seen a small picture on some website somewhere—and barely knew a thing about her.

While Marjorie bought herself a drink, Lena filled me in on how their strange friendship formed.

"I heard that he had a new girlfriend, but I didn't know who she was," Lena said. "Just that she was a girl he had met at work."

"Yeah, they got hired at the same time." I remembered that, at least.

"Well, Marj is cool. She's not what I expected."

Marjorie returned to our table with her own tall mocha. "This is too funny! Zack's three exes, all together."

Zack's TWO exes, but never mind.

"Sorry," Marjorie said. "You were saying?"

"Lena said you weren't what she expected."

"Oh, that's so true. *She* wasn't what I was expecting either. I kind of thought that Lena would be more like me, you know? I thought Zack had a type."

Looking at the two of them in front of me, I understood what they meant. Lena reminded me of college—all enthusiasm, spirit, pep, positivity.

Marjorie was reserved. I found her a bit serious, less quick to laugh, not too smiley. That didn't mean they were opposites, just that they were very different.

I noticed there was an ease between them that I didn't feel. "But you're friends now. Maybe you're not so different."

Lena laughed. "Oh, we almost have nothing in common. Believe me, we tried. Apart from yoga and Zack, we have nothing."

"We can't even go to movies together." Marjorie smiled, after faking a frustrated look. "It was interesting getting to know Lena, though. Because Zack *never* talked about her."

"Well, he talked about *Jasmine* a lot," Lena said.

"Totally," Marjorie added. "I knew all about that boss you hated, that work stalker you tried to avoid... and I heard all about you and Tim."

Me and Tim?

But Marjorie was obviously still on the subject. "I knew what was happening between you and Tim from when he first asked you out—to that basketball game. You two fought a lot too. I felt like Zack was telling me about a new fight every two weeks."

Why are they dragging this all out? "I broke up with Tim a long time ago. So what you know, Marjorie, is old news."

"The point is," she replied, "Why would Zack care so much about you and this guy? You and Zack broke up *in high school.* And still, we followed your relationship's ups and downs like it was a telenovela."

"See, it's not just me," Lena said. "Marjorie agrees."

"Zack is totally in love with you," Marjorie said, dead serious. "He'll end it with Kimmy if you ask him to."

"I'm not going to *ask* him to do that!"

Marjorie arched her eyebrows. "Really? You don't remember what you did for me five years ago?"

SIX

Five years ago

WHILE LENA and other people from college disappeared from my radar after grad, Zack did not.

He still lived in his parents' house, ten minutes from mine, and we both found work in Makati a few months out of school. He took a car to work, and I rode with him when I woke up early enough.

If I had changed after four years of college, so did he. Especially since he got a job at a big company that distributed food and soap and stuff. He was suddenly required to wear a nice shirt and tie every day, and he needed a car because he had to visit supermarkets in different areas of the city.

I, on the other hand, became the HR girl people submitted résumés to. I didn't mind working from the ground up. My day mostly consisted of sifting through emails and screening walk-in applicants, scheduling tests and interviews, and ushering people to and from waiting rooms.

At the pharma company, I had my own little group. We HR assistants (three girls and a guy) sort of banded together because we disliked our boss *so* much. We had lunch together, and maybe even caught a movie after work. But I still had my morning and early evening car rides with Zack.

I looked forward to them. I was proud of Zack. He was looking more professional and grown-up every day.

"I'm proud of you too," he said, quickly deflecting any extra attention. "And I think as soon as you get a good offer, you should leave your office."

"I've only been there a few months!"

"I mean, learn as much as you can, and then find another place where your boss won't keep you down doing photocopying and stuff. You have a talent for... for *reading* people, and you should become a more important part of the hiring process."

What he said was true, but that was the difference between his industry and mine. He was with a batch of ambitious people, all his age, all wanting better opportunities. I was pretty much a part of an assembly line. How long would it take for me to actually influence how a company hired people?

That might take forever. But I liked what I was doing, so I didn't mind if I wasn't on a fast track.

I studied psychology in college, but that only gave an academic background to what I really liked: analyzing people. I thought that I'd have to be a guidance counselor in a high school or something to practice it as a career, but then I ended up in an interesting place, Human Resources. And I've been fascinated by what I've seen so far. It's all about studying people and their behavior. Why do certain people work well together, and some don't? Why do some people who make horrible decisions in their personal lives make excellent executives? Why do some people think that being timid in an interview will get them hired?

I looked at these people who passed through my desk. From names on résumés, they became employees, and eventually I started seeing the effects of their personalities on the workplace. Some were good decisions, others not so. But Zack was right. I liked to *read* people. Whether or not that would lead to a high-powered career, I wasn't sure yet. Not in my first year on the job anyway.

This nice little carpool routine of ours continued for a few months. Zack's work schedule became a little more erratic, and then he got assigned to visit supermarkets in Laguna, and for a few weeks I didn't see him at all.

That was when I ran into an old friend in Glorietta. Ramon, Zack's friend and my PE ballroom dancing partner.

"Hi!" I beamed, genuinely happy to see him.

"How are you? You work with Zack right?"

"Yeah, Batch Four," Ramon said. He probably meant the fourth batch of their office's management trainee program, as if that meant anything to me.

"Zack got Laguna duty this time. We don't see him anymore."

"Yeah, neither do I."

Ramon remembered the girl he was standing next to and introduced me to her. "Jasmine Salazar, Marjorie Pineda. I went to college with Jasmine. Marjorie is from Batch Four too."

I shook her hand. Marjorie's handshake felt very...official. Add that to her smart corporate ensemble and she looked every inch the career girl that I should have been.

My handshake felt flimsy in comparison, and I was a little insecure about it.

"Oh!" Ramon's eyes widened as he remembered an interesting detail about me. "Jasmine is Zack's ex."

I recoiled unconsciously. I hadn't been referred to as Zack's ex in a long time, and the stress of having to maintain the lie returned. "Ramon, that was ages ago..."

Marjorie definitely looked interested and wasn't going to let it go. "Wow. Is she?"

"Why don't you ask her about the thing? It's okay for you to talk about Zack, right, Jasmine?" Ramon asked me.

Did I have a choice? "Uh, sure."

Marjorie hesitated, but Ramon prodded her to continue anyway. "It's just that...I kind of want to ask Zack to our Christmas party."

Déjà vu. Marjorie apparently liked Zack. Of course, because he was great.

However, word had gone around that Zack was unfortunately still hung up on his ex, and had not dated anybody since breaking up with her years ago.

"What does this have to do with me?" I asked.

Marjorie turned to Ramon for support, and then back to me. "Is it you? Are you the ex he isn't over yet?"

"*No,*" I said emphatically. "You probably mean Lena. They broke up in third year."

Ramon was confused. "I thought you two got back together in college?"

"*No we did not,*" I groaned.

"Still, you're probably closer to him than any of us. If there's anyone Marjorie should ask about this, it's you," he said.

True to form, Zack never talked to many people—not even to Ramon—about deeply personal stuff. So what

Ramon wanted me to do was to talk to Zack, and sort of *bring up* the idea of going to the Christmas party with Marjorie. Just to see what he thought.

"You want me to ask him out for you?" I couldn't believe this.

"I just want to see if he's open to it. If he isn't, then I won't ask him, no harm done. I don't want to rush him if he's heartbroken or something," Marjorie explained. "Ramon says you two are really close. It would be easier if you mentioned it first, right?"

I shook my head at Ramon. "And you can't do this yourself?"

"I wouldn't know how, Jas."

"And I wouldn't trust him to do it right," Marjorie added.

ZACK FINALLY GOT out of Laguna duty a week later, so on the first day back on his regular schedule, he picked me up at home.

"Yay!" I said happily, sliding into the passenger seat. "I have a car again! How was Laguna?"

"Interesting. I hope they reimburse my gas money soon."

"I saw Ramon in Glorietta, by the way."

"Cool. It's been a while since you've seen him, right?"

"Graduation probably. Zack...have you been...I don't know, have you seen Lena lately?"

"Lena?" He seemed surprised that I brought her up. "No."

"I was wondering if you were thinking of finally dating other people. It's been years since Lena."

"You think I don't think about that?" He was amused. "I think about it all the time."

"Hello, it's not obvious. The only date you have is your monthly visit to the comic book store." That was true, by the way. "Why don't you ask someone out?"

"Jasmine, what is this really about?"

I turned to him and smiled, hoping that even with his peripheral vision (his eyes were on the road) he would still see that I was only saying this because I cared about him. "I mean, I think you should start dating again. No more excuses."

"Yes, ma'am."

"I'm serious, Zack. You can't still be sad over Lena."

"I'm not. I'm really not."

"In that case..." I sucked in my breath and hoped this would work, "how do you feel about Marjorie?"

"Marjorie?"

"Marjorie Pineda. Your officemate."

"She's... she's okay."

"I think you should ask her out, on a friendly date or something. Like to your office Christmas party."

"How do you even *know* Marjorie?"

"When I bumped into Ramon, I met Marjorie. She's pretty and smart. I think you should ask her out."

"Did Ramon put you up to this?" he asked, his hands tightening around the steering wheel for a second. Suddenly I got worried. Zack had a strange relationship with his friends. Like he said, no single person knew that much about him. I didn't want him angry at Ramon over this.

"No he didn't," I said. Which wasn't a complete lie. "I happened to meet them, that's all. So why not Marjorie?"

He couldn't answer that, of course. There was no

reason, really, and he didn't give any. He exhaled–sounded like a sigh of exhaustion–and I wondered if a Monday morning was the wrong time to bring this up.

"So this is what you're saying," he said. "You want me to start dating other people again and you think this new person you met is right for me? This person you don't even know."

"But you know her. Why not her?"

There was a really long pause. I hoped he wasn't getting mad at me, and I suddenly wished I had been more subtle. Why did I have to be the only person who could talk to him like this? Ugh.

"You're right," he said, finally. "I've been making excuses not to date. Yeah, the Christmas party would be a safe time to start."

AS ZACK'S relationship with Marjorie went from Christmas party date to more than that, I saw less of him. But he still tried to offer me a ride to work once a week. That was sweet. Those car rides felt remarkably short too. The more time we spent apart, the more stories we tried to cram in that forty minute drive.

And then my love life started getting interesting.

I met Tim Gonzales at the pharma company. He was applying for a position in the marketing department, and I knew right away that he was going to get it. Few people *sauntered* into the HR waiting room like he did. Applicants were usually nervous, but not him.

On that first meeting, he found out we went to rival colleges–and he promptly invited me to the next big basketball game.

"Are you sure?" I asked. "What if you guys lose?"

"Doesn't matter. Best team always wins anyway," he said, cockily.

He walked out of there with a date—and eventually, the job. Type A personalities tended to do that.

SEVEN

Coffee shop, present day

MARJORIE WAS RIGHT. I did forget what I had done for her five years ago.

"But I didn't do it for *you*," I tried to protest. "I wanted what was best for Zack. He was such a loner at the time."

"Interesting you would say that," Lena said. "Didn't Zack have a lot of friends?"

"None that he really talked to. I mean, for a time there we didn't even know when his birthday was," Marjorie added.

They both looked at me like I had something to do with it.

"Jasmine," Lena said, pausing only to sip from her drink. "Why is this not obvious to you? Zack listens to you. He went out with Marjorie because you asked him to. He wasn't a loner if he had you."

"I don't have as much influence over him as you think! And besides, why should I even bother now? He hasn't talked to me in months. And *new girlfriend.* Fiancée. Why should I care?"

They looked at each other, and then Marjorie leaned forward. "I know that Kimmy is cheating on him," she whispered.

Kimmy Domingo was also part of Zack's Batch Four management trainee group. She and Marjorie were friends, or at least they used to be. This part of their history I wasn't so sure about. I only knew that he had been with Marjorie, they broke up, and then suddenly Kimmy was in the picture.

What really happened, Marjorie was quick to mention, was that Kimmy had started flirting with Zack in the last months of their relationship. It got to a point that Marjorie couldn't handle having to watch out for Kimmy and her antics.

"They'd get assigned to provincial site visits together," Marjorie complained. "Like, three times in a row! And the way we trainees were paired up was supposed to be *random.*"

"Why didn't you just trust him?" I asked.

Marjorie rolled her eyes. "Well of course *you* would have no problem trusting Zack. You never had to share. Lena and I, we had to go through it feeling like we were competing with memories of you. So there was that, and then Kimmy being Kimmy... I couldn't take it anymore." She shrugged, like she was shaking the unwanted thoughts from her head. "But anyway, that's over. I have a new boyfriend now and I have nothing but positive energy for Zack."

She continued her story: Kimmy and Zack got together a few months after he and Marjorie had broken up. It pretty much divided their group of friends—people sort of unconsciously chose sides, but Kimmy had probably meant to do it that way, to make sure that Marjorie and Zack didn't talk anymore.

So despite being officemates, Marjorie and Zack only saw each other a few times in the past year or so. Kimmy had completely monopolized his time.

That explains a lot, I thought.

Then Marjorie—randomly—got assigned to attend a conference with Kimmy, but by then she was dating another guy and only felt slightly awkward about it.

It took three days and the company paid for both girls to share a hotel room. Marjorie wasn't going to use it because her mom lived close to the hotel. The plans changed on the second night, though, when Marjorie got a little tipsy at dinner and didn't trust herself to drive home.

She still had her key to the room and decided to crash there. Instead, she walked in on Kimmy and some guy from the conference, in a rather compromising position. She quickly apologized and ran out—suddenly sober enough to drive.

The conference was two months ago. *After the wedding invitations were handed out*, I noticed.

"She was picking up guys in office conferences *three months* before her wedding!" Marjorie looked at me meaningfully. "You two don't know her, but this is classic Kimmy. I didn't think she'd still be doing this. And to *Zack*, of all people."

"You're sure she wasn't with Zack?" I asked.

Marjorie burst into laughter. "Yes, I'm sure. It was a different guy."

"I mean, did you really look?"

"Yes. He's totally hot but not Zack. I think I'd know what Zack looks like naked."

Lena shrugged. "I wouldn't."

"Neither would I," I said, then regretted it.

"No? Really?" Marjorie looked at us as if we were kidding. I definitely wasn't. "Anyway, I've debated with myself a zillion times about what to do with this information. Should I confront Kimmy or tell Zack? But I can't. If I tell Kimmy, she won't change, and she'll think I'm jealous. If I tell Zack, he won't believe me—and he'll probably think I'm bitter."

"I can't tell him," Lena said. "Because I haven't seen him in years. So we think you're the best person to do this. He's smart, but when it comes to girls he's just so dense sometimes. He doesn't deserve to be treated like this."

They were absolutely right. My heart sank a little, wondering if Zack knew about this. He had never talked to me about her. He never complained about his girlfriends. Was he suffering quietly or just clueless?

Lena and Marjorie were also right about the other thing. Neither of them was in a good position to tell Zack. An ex was not exactly the most objective messenger for this kind of news.

And how awful of me to even *think* of deserting him at a time like this. Sure, we weren't speaking now, and for that I totally blamed him, but that didn't mean I was going to refuse to help him.

When Tim and I broke up, he was there for me.

"Are you in?" Lena asked.

"Yes." I said. "He's lucky to have you two looking out for him."

"Or cursed," Marjorie laughed.

EIGHT

Four years ago

TIM and I broke up three times over three years.

Zack's joke was that we celebrated an anniversary by breaking up. I laughed the first time he said that, and then it happened again, and it stopped being funny.

What was our problem?

I like to describe it as his superiority complex. But that was too simple. Tim was incredibly sweet, fun, and thoughtful, when he remembered to be. When he wasn't that, he was condescending.

When I first introduced him to Zack over dinner, I could tell right away that they weren't going to get along. Zack had come alone (Marjorie had to work late) and right away I saw some kind of alpha male instinct activate in Tim. I thought guys would get along instantly if you threw them together and gave them beer, but for some reason these two defied expectations.

Zack was usually good with small talk. He found a

way to find something in common with people, and then kept going. He'd mention sports teams first. If that didn't work, then movies, then a TV show, then a recent big concert. Since Zack never shared stuff about his personal life, he tried to keep conversations limited to sports or pop culture.

If those didn't work, his last resort was to ask which school the person was from, and then hopefully they'd find a common friend. But he rarely used this unless he was totally comfortable and knew that he wasn't going to open a can of worms.

Tim, being a more social animal, skipped all steps and went straight for the name-dropping. "Oh, you work in ________? Do you know _______? What have you heard about ________? I heard this about _________ and maybe it's not true. Is it? Do you think _______ is worth the bonuses they give him?"

Not only that, he started to explain to Zack why I stuck around the office despite working for a boss I so disliked.

"Because she needs direction," he said, cocky smile on his face. "And he is able to give her that. He tells her what to do, and she does it well."

"That's bull," Zack retorted. "He's a micromanager and she's not learning anything from that. She doesn't have to stay with him any longer than she already has."

They both looked at me, both expecting me to agree. I smiled. "Well, I'm not quitting until I find a good replacement job."

When Tim excused himself to wash his hands, Zack leaned toward me and shook his head. "Is he always like this?"

"Like what?"

"Arrogant."

"He's not arrogant. He's...he just has a strong personality."

"And he happens to think you have a weak one."

"No he does not. Stop it." I wasn't as shy as I used to be, but compared to Type As like Tim, I sort of blended into the background.

Our dinner arrived, but Zack acted like he wasn't hungry. In fact, halfway through the dinner, he checked his phone and looked relieved when Marjorie needed him to pick her up.

"Nice meeting you, *pare*." Tim sent him off with a brisk handshake.

THREE YEARS ago

AFTER MY FIRST anniversary with Tim, I realized the root of our problems. He never stopped thinking of me as the HR girl who accepted his résumé and sent him to the waiting room.

As he thrived in our office and got more and more respect, he started to see himself moving up—but didn't see me going in the same direction. He had a way of talking down to me, or talking about me that belittled what I did, and that got old quickly.

I wanted to make the relationship work, but it wasn't going to change as long as we worked together.

So I quit and found another job.

Zack did *not* like this. He had always wanted me to find a better job and boss, but I had the feeling he didn't like my reasons.

It didn't matter anyway, because the way Tim treated

me didn't change. Even as I moved up from HR assistant to senior assistant to supervisor, he was still a jerk who thought he was much smarter than me and knew what was good for me.

LAST YEAR

THE THIRD AND final time I broke up with Tim was a few days after our third anniversary.

I think it started quite innocently. One minute he was driving me home, and the next we were in the middle of an old fight.

"Forget I said anything," I mumbled.

"What did he want now?"

"I don't know. He wanted to talk, okay? He does that. We're *friends*."

"Are you sure you're just friends?" There was a tense tone in his voice that I didn't like. Accusing.

"You've *met* the guy. Several times."

"That's not what Marco Chan says."

Marco was one of Tim's friends at the pharma company. "What are you talking about?"

"He went to college with you. He told me he was pretty sure that Zack is your ex."

Oh god why won't it go away? And I barely knew Marco. "That's not true."

"Jasmine," Tim said, pulling out that Tone of Condescension from somewhere in his diaphragm. "Why would Marco Chan lie to me about something like that?"

"I don't know!" I yelled back. I knew that this was when I should have come clean and let my boyfriend of three years know the truth, but...it wasn't worth it. I couldn't be bothered. "I'm just sick of having to explain this. He's not my ex. He was never my boyfriend. And if you want to believe this guy and not me, then I don't want to see you anymore."

That was a tough request and I knew it. Because that lie? It could be verified by dozens of people from college. The truth? Only Zack and I—and maybe our closest high school friends—knew this, and Tim was not going to take our word for it.

But I think I wanted to push him that far. I was done with him.

The fight started because I received a text message from Zack. He asked if I wanted a ride to work the next morning.

"*Sure,*" I texted back. I made the mistake of mentioning this to Tim, which unfortunately revived the argument we kept having about Zack and the amount of time he spent with me. Which was almost zero, by the third year of my relationship with Tim, not that he noticed. Between the new job, dates with Tim and everything else, I hadn't seen Zack that much.

Rather than drop me off at home and then leave, Tim decided that he wanted to stick around for a few hours and "reason" with me. I couldn't believe that I ever found this overbearing jerk attractive.

It was like our prior two breakups, which pretty much dissolved after hours of listening to him. But this time I didn't cave. I could feel in my bones that this breakup would stick. I felt relief was about to come.

He finally left the house past midnight, and I spent the early hours of the morning ignoring his calls. I did *not* look good at six-thirty AM, when Zack dropped by to pick me up.

"What happened?" He probably thought I was sick with something.

Despite the dark circles under my eyes, my fatigue from lack of sleep, and the rumbling in my stomach from skipping breakfast, I smiled. I snapped on the seat belt and said dramatically, "I broke up with Tim. Again."

"For real this time?"

"Yes." What a relief it was. If I only had a good night's sleep, I'd be happier.

"Are you okay?"

"Yes, I am more than okay."

"Why do you look like shit?"

"He kept calling and texting last night. I had to keep my phone on because it's my alarm clock. And I still overslept, so I hardly had enough time to shower and dress up before you arrived."

"I guess we both deserve a sick day then."

"Huh?"

"Text your boss that you're going on leave today."

At the next intersection, Zack stopped at the red light, and we both picked up our phones and sent "*I'm sick, be at work tomorrow*" messages to our bosses.

Why didn't I think of that? Was I really planning to go to work looking like a zombie?

Before the light turned green, we got our replies. "*Feel better*," was mine. And "*I didn't know Superman could get sick*" was his.

"Okay, that's a sign of overachievement," I said, laughing as I read the text.

I noticed that Zack kept driving north. "Where are we going?"

"Breakfast." He didn't say anything more.

In an hour and a half, we had left the parts of the city I

was familiar with. I only vaguely knew that we were on the road to Antipolo. He said there was this nice restaurant he had discovered, and hoped that it was open for breakfast. He found their number on his phone and called ahead.

I lost track of how many turns we took, driving on that winding road up the hill. Zack finally parked the car in front of what looked like a house.

Seconds later, I discovered it was built on top of the hill, converted into a bed and breakfast. We were the only customers, and a smiling middle-aged man led us to one of five tables in the dining room. We had a spectacular view of Manila from our seats.

Almost as soon as we sat down, the man brought plate after plate to our table. A small stack of waffles, an omelet (cheese, olives, onions), and bacon. A little pitcher of syrup, a saucer of butter, and a pot of tea soon followed.

As soon as I smelled the butter, my stomach rumbled. "When did we order?"

"When I called, I asked for the usual. It's better to call ahead. They usually take a long time cooking."

We dug into our breakfast, and I loved how sweet, salty, buttery, and bacon-fatty all blended together in my mouth in one disgusting, glorious bite. "How did you find this place?"

"My mom loves it here. She knows the woman who owns it."

"It's *amazing*." Even the weather was perfect. It was gorgeous and sunny—almost daring me to feel sad. "Thank you for taking me here. And this is classic comfort food breakfast, so awesome."

"I know what you like," he said. "So what made you finally end it?"

"I realized that I was sick of him. You knew that though, right?"

"I hated him the first time I met him."

"But you weren't being fair."

"Well, it's done, so I'm happy that you came to your senses."

Only Zack understood how liberating my decision was. He seemed genuinely happy for me, which was nice. The two of us were a funny pair, in our corporate outfits, a little overdressed for the quaint bed and breakfast.

"I always knew you deserved better."

We stayed there for a few more hours and watched the sun move up in the sky, finishing off the fresh fruits they served us to cap the meal. As it neared noon, it became unbearably hot so we drove back down to Manila. By early afternoon, I was back at home, sprawled on my bed, finally getting some rest.

FUNNY how easy it was to cut a Tim-sized chunk out of my life and have it continue generally the same way.

Looking back, moving to a different company was good not just for my career, but for my breakup as well. No longer two floors up, Tim dropped out of my life without much trouble. After a month he stopped calling, and after another month, I stopped "accidentally" running into him on my way to and from work.

He was probably checking if I had gotten together with Zack, which was always his suspicion.

That wasn't a problem for me. Zack had gone back to his usual erratic schedule and we didn't see each other more than once a week (when he'd offer a ride to work).

At work, I got assigned to do something I was *really* interested in—administering the Myers-Briggs Type Indicator test on all of the BPO's employees. I was familiar with it from college as the test that told people if they were ENFP (Extraversion, Intuition, Feeling, Perceiving) or ISTJ (Introversion, Sensing, Thinking, Judging) and various combinations thereof. It was fun as a personality test in college, but this was that on a grander scale.

Imagine being able to, in Zack's words, *read* all these people. And not just that, but give them insight that might actually help them get along better with their teammates. That was when I started to enjoy going to work every day.

Worrying about Tim or wondering where Zack was sort of faded into the background.

SIX MONTHS ago

"SURE I'LL WATCH a movie with you," I said.

"When?"

"Tonight?"

Zack sprung the movie invite on me as I stepped out of the car.

"I get off work at seven."

"Last full show then?"

"Okay."

I was in the middle of a project, so I made a note on my calendar so I wouldn't forget.

Wednesday – Movie with Z.

Four weeks later and that calendar had at least two "*Movie with Z*" or "*Dinner with Z*" notes a week.

That was out of the ordinary, and I didn't even stop to

think about it until a month later. Don't get me wrong, I appreciated it. I had almost forgotten what it was like to *have plans* after work.

Over dinner on Friday night, I watched him as we ate and thought about how to interrogate him. Surely he was going through something—our friendship since college was never this regular. He really took his "free agent" persona to heart, but I noticed that he would seek the company of friends when he felt down. Not that he'd tell them what was bothering him.

At this point, Zack had evolved yet again—no more sloppily-ironed shirts, no ill-fitting pants, no scuffed shoes. Even his hair went through a change, now mostly off his forehead with non-greasy-looking hair product.

I wondered if someone helped him change. It was like he had discovered what looked and felt good, and it now showed in the way he dressed. Ratty T-shirt Zack was gone.

"What's up with you?" I asked bluntly.

My tone was more of a "What's your problem?" than "How are you?" so he frowned at me defensively.

"What do you mean?" he said.

"You and I have been meeting too regularly," I explained. "Which never really happens unless you're... I don't know, unless something's up. So what's wrong?"

"What, so I can't hang out with my friend Jasmine if I want to?" Zack made a show of dropping his utensils and pretending to leave.

"You'd tell me if you were in trouble, right?" I was a little concerned now. "Like, if you're sick or something."

"You're overreacting," Zack said. "And paranoid. I'm not sick. If I were, you'd know because you'll be changing my bed pan."

"That's what happens when you keep your friends at a

distance," I scolded lightly. "None of them will want to help dispose of your pee."

I still felt I was on to something though, despite Zack's denials.

"Is Tim still bothering you?" Zack asked.

Now this was even more classic. Whenever Zack was going through something, he became more sensitive to *my* problems. It was like he was racking up good karma points for himself by being nice to others.

"He finally stopped texting," I said, indulging him. "And waiting for me at the lobby of my building. Which is a good thing because if he saw us together, there would be *so* much drama."

Zack flashed me a look of smugness. "If I had known that seeing us together would make him snap, I would have made plans with you a long time ago. Have you started dating again?"

"No," I admitted. "My calendar lately is full of work. And you."

"Yeah, you shouldn't rush it if you're not ready."

And then he gave me a big smile, one I hadn't seen in a long time. "It's not like I'm wasting your time, right? You get a social life and free meals! I, in fact, am your savior."

"I'm wasting *some* time," I teased. "Two of those movies you wanted to see were crap."

"If you had more beer like I did, you would have had more fun."

"Yes, watching movies intoxicated is *very* mature."

"Cheers!" He lifted his bottle and toasted my glass of iced tea.

The movie we watched that night was an Oscar contender and it was the slowest, most painfully pretentious period movie I had ever seen.

But Zack loved it.

"Anthony Hopkins is so funny!" he kept saying, poking my side. "Did you know he was so funny?"

He *wasn't* funny. At least not in the movie.

"Okay, no driving for you," I said, taking his keys. I didn't have a car but I learned how to drive because Zack helped me practice. Despite already being licensed, I didn't drive often. But when I did, I remembered senior year in college, learning to drive in Zack's dad's car.

When Zack got his own car, he almost never let me drive.

"Nothing personal," he said, when it was new. "But I'm actually paying for this with my own money."

Surprisingly, he let me push him into the passenger seat without much protest. Zack liked to drink but I never saw him *pissed* (in the British sense) and it was interesting. Because, apparently, he didn't get rude or violent or obnoxious.

He got *talkative*. And found everything funny.

"I've always wanted to be a director," he suddenly declared, totally without context, as I drove out of the mall parking building.

"No shit?" I said, laughing. "Where did that come from?"

"My dream movie project," he continued, "is adapting Neil Gaiman's *1602*. Years ago, I wanted to do either a political war period piece action movie or a superhero movie and then I read *1602* and suddenly I thought, *shit*, why can't I do both?"

I decided to humor him. "I didn't know you wanted to be a filmmaker."

"I don't. I'm sure I'll suck at it. I want it to be done and I want to go around promoting it, but I don't want to do it. You know?"

I laughed. "Yes I know. All the credit and none of the work."

"Exactly. Making a movie is too hard. It takes *years,* right? And then the final product is two hours long. Unless you make an epic."

"Do you want to make an epic?"

"Only epics are worth watching," he said, eyes glazing over but tone totally serious. "Two hours of people sitting and talking—that is not a real movie. Explosions! Costumes! Drama! That is a movie."

"Wow. I think I like you like this, Zack. A little alcohol and I get a lot of blackmail material."

"I'm not drunk," he insisted. "I'm letting you drive so you can feel *empowered*. My life is in your hands."

I never thought of it that way. All those times I put *my* life in his hands.

In the fifteen minutes that it took me to drive to his house, he told me three other movie plots he would direct if he got the chance.

Had I ever seen him drunk before? No. Did he drink a lot that night? I didn't think he drank *that* much. It was a good thing I managed to bring him home without incident, hand him into the custody of his brother, and take his car home.

I drove it back the next morning.

"You didn't have to do this," he said, meeting me at his front door, sober and sleepy. "I was going to drop by your house to get it."

"It's okay. I was on my way to the gym." I went to a gym nearby on Saturday mornings.

"Well... do you need a ride to the gym then?"

I laughed. He had answered the door in the same outfit he was wearing the night before, and it looked like he was struggling to stay alert. "No thank you. You get some sleep. I'll see you soon."

"Thanks, Jas." He probably realized how he looked and smiled sheepishly. "Do you want to come in? I think there's food."

"Gym, remember?"

"Right." Zack took the keys from me. "So that's it?"

"Yes. I'm going to go now."

"Okay." Then he stepped forward, and kissed me on the lips. It was a quick, undramatic, almost half-hearted kiss, the way a couple of several years would say goodbye to each other.

"Whoa," I said, jumping back before it got a little more...*un*-platonic than that. "Um, okay. I have to go."

I got out of there quickly. I didn't stay long enough to see if he had realized what he had done.

And that, for the record, regardless of what anyone else says, was my first kiss with Zack.

THAT AFTERNOON, I was surprised to get a text from Ramon. "*You going tonight?*"

I didn't think and automatically replied,

"*Where?*"

"*My birthday. I emailed you last week.*"

Whoops. I vaguely remembered an invite to a restaurant in Serendra, but probably messed up on the date. "*Sure, yes I'll be there,*" I texted back. I didn't discuss that at all with Zack but I was almost sure he'd be there, and I kind of wanted to see him too.

What was with that kiss? I wondered as I decided what to wear. *And the recent invites? Is he actually...? No that's just Zack being Zack.*

I chose a new blue dress (the skirt fell conservatively below my knees but it was cut a little lower along the neckline), spent more than the usual minutes on my hair, and hopped into a cab that took me to Ramon's birthday dinner.

And I was nervous.

Why are you nervous, Jas? It's like you think Zack likes you or something.

He doesn't.

He's just being Zack.

The guests were mostly from work, but there were a few from college—and most of them I actually knew, so I wasn't entirely out of place. We didn't even have to mingle; his college friends were at one table, and work friends were at another.

It was nice catching up with college friends. Or technically, Zack and Ramon's friends. They were a cool group, and I didn't exactly get to hang out with them a lot. It was interesting to find out what they had done with their lives since we had graduated over four years ago.

Zack didn't arrive until an hour later, and boy did he make an entrance.

I didn't know what made the whole thing more surreal: That Zack arrived with a tall, curvaceous girl in a dress that was a size too small for her, or that *no one else thought it was unusual but me.*

"Zack! Kimmy!" Ramon said, pleased to see them both.

I instinctively ducked, hiding behind the guy sitting next to me, as I watched Zack and this Kimmy. He was holding her hand, and the length of her body was pressing comfortably against him.

Too comfortably.

That's his girlfriend, I realized, suddenly feeling nauseous.

Like usual, he never said anything. Never talked about having a girlfriend. Or not having a girlfriend. For *weeks* we were hanging out. Watching movies. Not a word about this.

Zack being Zack.

What does that make me?

They took seats at the work table right away, so I managed to watch them for a few more minutes without being discovered.

This "Kimmy" definitely acted like a girlfriend. Once they were seated, she idly rested a hand on Zack's thigh. She seemed to be familiar with his work friends, because she was participating actively in their conversation instead of politely listening. Other times she would lean forward and gently touch Zack's ear, or hair, or shoulder, and when she laughed, she angled herself toward him. Possessively.

She looked nothing like Marjorie. Or Lena.

This Kimmy was what other people would call a bombshell. Everything about her—hair, body, clothes—was fabulous, and she knew it.

Where was she this whole month?

The food was good, but I couldn't eat it. I felt...

I felt humiliated.

"Jasmine's here," I heard Ramon say, and my spine froze.

I was taught this in General Psych—they called it the cocktail party effect. It's when you are almost inexplicably able to hear someone say your name even in a crowded place, even when you are not being spoken to directly. Like at a cocktail party, when you are somehow able to hear the person you're talking to despite everyone else talking around you.

In this case it wasn't that inexplicable. I may have been at the other table but I knew they'd get around to me eventually.

Zack was, to put it simply, surprised. I saw him whip his head around, looking for me, and I merely raised an eyebrow as a response.

He was able to get his composure back in a second, and then stood up, dragging Kimmy with him.

"Hey," he said.

Everyone at the table said hi, but he was looking directly at me.

"Hi," I said.

"Jasmine, this is Kimmy."

They look good together, I had to admit. Zack had always been cute, but I guess I still thought of him as my college buddy. Seeing him with Kimmy opened my eyes to how other people probably saw him now—as part of a power couple. It was as if he suddenly aged ten years in my mind that moment.

She smiled at me, flashing her white teeth. "Oh, so *you're* Jasmine."

I shook her hand. "Hi, Kimmy."

"I've heard so much about you," she gushed.

"That's what they all say," I said curtly.

Zack smiled politely and moved on to the other people at the table. He didn't speak to me privately that night. I didn't hear from him after that.

Two weeks later, I received their wedding invitation in the mail.

NINE

Coffee shop, present day

"HOLY SHIT!" Marjorie declared.

I told them the short version of what had happened. That Zack suddenly started seeing me a lot, not mentioning at all that he had a new girlfriend. I concluded with the last time I saw him at Ramon's birthday dinner.

I did not tell them about the kiss because that would just tangle with whatever they thought they knew about me and Zack.

Lena didn't know any of this either. "So wait...you didn't even know he and Marjorie had broken up?"

I shook my head. "No. I don't know what kind of friendship you think we have, but we don't really talk about you two."

Marjorie snapped her fingers. "That's why she got him to propose to her!"

"What?" I said.

Marjorie groaned. "Kimmy is motivated when she's threatened. She's like that at work, and it makes sense that she's like that with Zack. She usually treats him like crap except when she feels that someone might take him away from her."

"You think he hung out with me only to make her jealous?" I felt my face going red, ten years of progress with my self-esteem going down the drain.

Lena put a hand on my arm. "We don't know that. We know he likes you by default."

Marjorie shrugged. "Unless he was telling Kimmy that he was seeing you when they weren't together. But who knows?"

"Then they deserve each other," I spat, starting to feel angry on top of feeling betrayed.

"Wait," Lena, obviously the more romantic of Zack's two exes, said. "Think about this. It's possible that their relationship was going bad and Zack was *running to you* for help."

"He never said anything," I grumbled.

"But that's always been his problem, right? He never says anything. Not even when it's important."

"This is what I think happened," Marjorie said. "Kimmy was treating him like crap. So he was thinking of breaking up with her, but rather than actually doing it which would have made sense, he started to reconnect with you, Jasmine. Then when you all see each other at Ramon's dinner, Kimmy suddenly sees how hot you are."

"Your reasoning is flawed," I pointed out. "Kimmy is a supermodel. She will not be intimidated by me."

Marjorie looked at Lena. "Has she always been this clueless?"

Lena smiled knowingly. "Yes. And she's supposed to be a psych major too."

"Jasmine, trust me, you are beautiful. Sure, not the way Kimmy's got all the height and smoking bod, but she's heard enough stories about you to know that you totally *get* Zack, intellectually, emotionally, and stuff. Plus you have all that history."

I wanted to contradict her but Lena gave me a look that shut me up.

Marjorie continued, "She comforted herself with the knowledge that because she's all fabulous and sexy, Zack will never leave her. Then she finally met you and realized what Lena and I did years ago."

"What is that?"

"That you are *exactly* who Zack wants."

Cognitive dissonance is when your mind is unable to accept two contradictory ideas and is quite bothered about letting both ideas exist at the same time. Sometimes the brain selects only the thing it can process and ends up creating its own warped version of reality. That's what I was feeling right then.

For almost ten years I had pretty much trained myself to ignore what people said about me and Zack. Because these people *had no idea what they were talking about.* If they actually believed that I was Zack's ex, then nothing they said applied. It was like their words existed in this alternate reality that I pretended to live in.

But all of a sudden, I *wished* that what Marjorie said was true. I knew she was basing it on a false assumption, and was most likely wrong, but...

If she knew that I was never Zack's ex, would she and Lena have come to the same conclusion?

Would they still think that this girl Zack kept talking about was someone he was in love with, or just a friend?

I *wanted* it to be true, though. So badly that it took me by surprise.

That's why you felt you were punched in the gut when you saw him with Kimmy. That's why you hadn't been able to call him since you got the wedding invitation.

Oh, God, I was in love with Zack. No matter what Lena and Marjorie believed, I at least knew how I felt. And it was a horrible thing to feel one month before his wedding.

"I don't know if he still wants me," I said slowly. "But I've got to tell him how I feel."

"You're in?" Lena asked.

"So what do I do?"

TEN

Setting up a dinner date with a newly engaged Zack was harder than it used to be.

Then again, I never did the inviting before, so I didn't know how he'd respond to my sudden invitation.

"Sorry, busy," he kept saying, over and over again. If it wasn't a work thing, it was a wedding-related thing like a fitting, or a meeting with the caterers. I tried skipping the text message and giving him a call, but it was rejected, with an apologetic text quickly following: "*Sorry in meeting.*"

The date of his wedding neared and I started to panic. Or rather, I alternated between sleepless panicking and exhausted resignation.

"It's no use," I told Lena over the phone, after my third day of trying to get Zack to meet me. For three days, I had been ready to leave work and go straight to dinner with him, but so far no go. "He's busy."

"He's avoiding you!" Lena's shrill voice was almost too loud. "You can't give up!"

"Send me Marjorie's number," I said.

Marjorie, it turned out, didn't know where he was

either. She was on a different floor and didn't see him on a daily basis, but she could find out if she really had to. As I waited for her update, I pretended to work and felt resignation creep in again.

This was silly. Maybe Zack didn't need me to save him. Why would he? He never said anything, never gave any indication that he was unhappy.

Except for those times when I suspected there was something he wasn't telling me.

But why not tell me? Why keep it to himself?

Maybe it was best that this never happened.

Zack and I had been friends for a long time. Why change it now? How was I even going to start talking to him about all of this?

"I found out where he is. Be at lobby of the Summit building in ten minutes!" was Marjorie's text message to me five minutes later.

I got there in eight; it was only a few blocks away. The row of elevators was bringing people to the lobby in batches, and all of them brushed past me, the girl who didn't seem to be in a rush to go anywhere.

Zack emerged from one of the elevators a few minutes later. Not what I expected. I thought he had been in a client meeting, but he was wearing jeans and a plain white shirt, a duffel bag was slung over his shoulder, and his hair was damp.

He came from the gym. When did Zack start going to a gym?

My mind flashed back to Zack in college, how he looked after a basketball game with his friends. Sometimes he'd offer to drive me home but I had to wait for their game to end, and he always met me fresh from a shower. Of course he was going to the gym. That explained why his shirts fit a little better, the muscle definition in his arms...

"Zack!" I called, almost letting him get away.

"Jas," he said, and the way he said my name, letting the "s" run a little long, as he always did, made a nervous thrill run up my neck. "Hi. Why are you here?"

"I met a friend over there," I lied, pointing to the restaurant in the lobby. "And I just got out. Since when do you go to the gym?"

He brought a hand up to his hair self-consciously. "A few months now. It's fun. Really clears my head."

Another batch of people from the elevator started to walk around us, rushing to get out of the building. Zack looked like he was halfway out the door himself, but was probably waiting for me to say something.

"Are you finally free for dinner tonight?" I blurted out.

"But you already had dinner."

"Um, no that was... I just had coffee."

I don't know what kind of desperation was there in my eyes, but a moment later he shrugged and agreed.

OKAY, *how exactly am I supposed to do this?* I couldn't just say, *Don't marry Kimmy!* I should at least ask him about his family first. So that was how we spent most of the time talking about his brother Gerard and his wife Ria who had given birth to a baby boy they were naming Greg after his *lolo*. I also ended up telling him about my job and how I was actually enjoying it.

Before I knew it, we were almost done with dinner so I just blurted out, "How's Kimmy?"

"She's fine."

"Wedding plans going okay?"

"I'm not aware of many of the details, but so far, no problems with the stuff I'm in charge of."

Is he holding out on me? Or are Lena and Marjorie making me paranoid?

"I never got to thank you for my invitation," I said.

He shrugged, almost too casually. "Yeah, well, it's a big moment, right? You have to be there."

"Are you ready for it?"

"For what?"

"For marriage."

He smiled tightly. "I'm marrying her, aren't I?"

"I don't know. I think we're young, that's all."

"When my parents got married my dad was twenty-three. I'm older than that now. No one's telling me I'm too young to do this."

"Well weren't they together for five years before they got married?"

"What does that mean?"

I felt a chill invade our warm, comfortable dinner, but there was no way to stop it.

Here goes... "I don't think you know Kimmy very well."

He pushed himself back against his chair, his face registering annoyance. I suddenly got the feeling that this wasn't the first time he had been told this.

"I thought at least you would be *happy* for me."

"How can I?" I hissed, trying to keep my voice down. "I meet this girl for two minutes and then find out that you're marrying her? What am I supposed to feel?"

"Nothing. I expect you to be the way you normally are and not feel anything," he said.

"Are you sure about this wedding, Zack?"

He looked at me in disbelief. "Jasmine, *this wedding* is

happening twenty days from now. Of course I'm sure. I haven't heard from you since I sent you that invitation and you talk to me about this *twenty days before the wedding?*"

"Are you kidding me? You make it sound like *I've* been avoiding *you*! I have dinner with you every time you ask, and *I* don't even get a courtesy visit when you deliver the invites?"

I had never, ever asked Zack to explain himself like this. Not when he made me lie to Lena, not when they broke up, not whenever he needed me to be the Jasmine from our imaginary relationship. I was always on his side, and I never confronted him about anything. Until now.

He folded his arms, not at all yielding to me. "Is that it? Are you mad because I didn't deliver the invite *in person?*"

Wrong! Why is he being so stubborn? "That's not what—Zack, I was told something about Kimmy that I think you should know." I had one card left.

"What can you possibly know about Kimmy that I don't?"

"She slept with someone at a work conference a few months ago."

It was a horrible thing to say, and I knew it, and it was ten times so much more horrible as soon as I saw what it did to his face. The way he looked at me. Why did I think I could do this? Why did I think...?

Zack clenched his hand into a fist and laid it down on the table. I jumped a little in my seat, thinking he'd slam it down, but he didn't. "How can you...why would you tell me that?"

It was there and I had to run with it. "But it's true."

He shook his head. "I can't believe I'm hearing this. I expected this from other people, but not from you. You don't even know Kimmy. I thought you'd give her a chance. She's changed."

"So you don't believe she cheated on you?"

"Jas, whatever problems Kimmy and I had, we're beyond that. I'm supposed to completely trust her."

But he wasn't saying that Kimmy didn't cheat.

Because you know all this but you're deciding to stay with her anyway.

"And it doesn't bother you that even after she asked you to completely trust her, she cheated on you anyway? With some random guy she had probably just met?"

"What do you want me to do, Jas?" he said, frustration creeping into his voice. "I'm getting married."

"You don't have to go through with it. This is the rest of your life, Zack. Are you sure this will make you happy?"

"It'll get better."

"What if it doesn't?" I insisted, covering his fist with my hand. "You shouldn't get married because you *hope* it'll get better."

"Really. And you're saying I do what? Call it off? Throw away all that money, disappoint all my relatives, and break Kimmy's heart? Is that what you want me to do?"

I felt his fist clench again, anger building up under his skin. I gripped his fist tighter and held it down on the table. "Zack, I want you to be happy. You shouldn't care about disappointing anybody."

I watched him let out his breath, and hoped he was actually thinking about it. I moved my hand, but he grabbed it and held on to it before I could pull away. "Jasmine."

"What?"

"Who told you to talk to me about this?"

"Nobody." His grip on my hand was like iron, and his fingers were cold. It was the first time he had held my hand with any kind of intensity, and it was a little scary. Not that I felt unsafe, but I knew I could say something that could totally undo him.

This could be it. This could be when we finally told each other the truth, about everything.

Marjorie and Lena put me up to this.

I want to know if you're in love with her.

I want to know if you ever loved me.

I love you right now.

It was hard. I wasn't used to it.

He said this and it sounded like he was begging. "Please. I don't see you for months and now you tell me that you *'heard'* things about Kimmy. Who put you up to this?"

"*I* put myself up to this. I care about you." That, and I wasn't going to rat on the people who cared enough about him to find me and convince me to do something this drastic.

"You don't know what my relationship with Kimmy is like," he said, his voice struggling to stay controlled. "None of my friends do. So if any of them asked you to do this, you shouldn't really believe everything they say."

"I don't care about what they say. But don't do this if you're not sure. Please."

He pulled my hand to him and I leaned forward, bringing me almost to his face. "Do you really know me, Jasmine?"

Do I?

My brain complied, flashing memories I had of Zack.

"I think so," I whispered.

"Then you know that no one knows every single thing about me," he said quietly. "If any of my friends asked you to break up my wedding, they don't know the whole story.

I'm not leaving Kimmy because someone started a rumor and asked you to tell me about it."

"Zack," I pleaded, "It's not just about what she *did* at the conference. This has to be a pattern of behavior, right? Never a one-time thing. Don't even break up with her if you still love her, but maybe...maybe talk to her first. Getting married is a serious step."

He shook his head and let go of my hand. "I think you forget that you were never my girlfriend," he said. "What gives you the right to meddle in my life?"

Zack waited for me to answer. I didn't. Couldn't.

He left money on the table—more than enough to cover dinner—and left.

ELEVEN

Five years ago

WHEN I REALIZED I was in love with Zack, it started to mess with my memories. Simple events became evidence of that deeper connection I felt I had with him, and it was hard for me to separate what was real and what wasn't.

On college graduation day, I was a mess. My original plan was to ride to school with my parents, but my mom had a work emergency so my dad had to wait for her.

I called Zack. "Where are you?" I yelled into the phone.

"Ten minutes. Just got off the highway."

"Ten minutes from school? I'm still home."

"What?"

"I was hoping I could ride with you, but if you're that close I'll get a cab instead."

"Wait for me, I'm turning the car around."

"No! Zack, it's okay, I'll get a cab."

"I said wait for me! Heading there now. You're not going to grad in a cab."

He made it to my house with half an hour to spare before the ceremonies started.

"I can't believe you came back," I said, catching my breath.

"You should've called me earlier," he replied, shaking his head.

Zack was dressed in the required semi-formal attire. He decided to go with what I recognized as his thesis-defense look—long-sleeved, pressed shirt, tie, black pants. I was wearing a new green dress, and my mom hired someone to do my hair and makeup.

"You look nice," Zack said.

"You ironed your shirt," I teased.

Zack's car screeched into an empty parking space five minutes after the ceremony officially started.

Plus he couldn't find parking near the auditorium, so we were probably five more minutes away from getting into the building. After we threw our robes on, he grabbed my hand and started running.

"I'm in heels!" I shrieked. "And slow down! I don't think we're going to miss anything!"

"*I* don't want you to miss anything," he said. "So hurry!"

When we entered the auditorium, the dean was giving a speech. Zack walked with me to find my assigned row.

"Thanks," I whispered, getting ready to take my seat.

"Congratulations," he said, kissing my forehead before running off to find his own seat with his Management classmates.

Three hours later, I was hugging my block mates, joking that all the hugging was because we were so happy the long ceremony was over. Everyone seemed emotional.

Zack caught up with me outside the auditorium and gave me a hug that lifted me off my feet.

"Congratulations to you too," I said, once my shoes touched the ground again.

"Why do I get the feeling this has happened before?" he asked.

That was funny, I felt that way too. "It's because we told people that we hugged at our high school graduation and you forgave me for dumping you at the prom."

"Oh right," he said, laughing. "And that didn't happen?"

"No."

"Well at least the good part did." He brought me close and hugged me again, and I felt him kiss the top of my head through my hair. "I'm glad we met here. I'm really sorry I didn't know you in high school."

"We made up for it," I said. "College would have been totally different if I didn't know you."

"I'm off to my family dinner. Do you need a ride?"

"No. The parents are here and I'm riding with them."

"Okay. I'll see you."

"Bye!" I waved at him.

When I turned around to look for my mom and dad, I saw Lena right behind me.

"Hey," she said. "I'm really happy for you."

"Um, congratulations to you too," I stammered, not sure what she meant.

She stepped toward me and gave me a hug.

Everyone's so touchy feely today, I thought.

But that memory had since been painted over with a different brush, and I wondered if I had it all wrong. Was I in love with Zack even then? Did he love me?

Because it looked like everyone knew it but us, and that made me want to cry.

TWELVE

Present day

IT WAS a bad day at work.

Three of the interviews I had scheduled had to be cancelled because the three company vice presidents who were supposed to do the interviews got called into an emergency meeting. First thing in the morning, I was frantically trying to reach the interviewees before they got to our office.

I managed to contact two out of the three—and dreaded having to tell the last one that she showed up for nothing.

A phone rang in the HR office, and the secretary picked it up.

"Jasmine?" Ms. Belinda called. "You have a visitor."

I checked my watch. Three-thirty. Expecting the applicant, I said, "Can you send her to the waiting room? I'll be with her in a minute."

While I prepared the forms, I heard the door to the waiting room open and close. I grabbed a black pen and walked over.

Waiting inside was Kimmy Domingo. She was sitting at the far end of the conference table, facing the door. The harsh fluorescent lights did nothing to diminish her beauty, and I couldn't help but notice her flawless, rosy skin.

Zack, couldn't you have chosen a girl who wouldn't easily crush my self-esteem with a stiletto heel?

"You're not the applicant," I said stupidly, stating the obvious.

She rolled her eyes, stood up, and easily towered over me even if I was in heels. "I don't appreciate what you did, Jasmine."

"What did I do?"

"You told Zack rumors about me?" Kimmy shook her head. "That's low."

"Are they true?"

Kimmy raised an eyebrow and sat down. "Does it matter, Jasmine?"

"What are you talking about?"

"What matters is if Zack believes you. I know your source of that rumor, and I also know that if it ever came out that she was the source, no one who knows me and Zack will ever believe it."

"Even if it's true?"

She shrugged, almost like she was humoring me. "It's her word against mine, and I know Zack trusts me."

Kimmy was unbelievable. There was her imposing, intimidating beauty, but there was also a restrained menace in her voice. Though she was seated and keeping her voice down, she was still able to bully me. I felt for Marjorie all of a sudden; I could totally see how she would find a girl like Kimmy a threat. Kimmy seemed to get her way all the time.

She and Tim are two of a kind, was the unbidden

thought that popped into my head. *But this is MY turf. There will be no bullying of me on my turf.*

"But you know Zack will believe me," I said pointedly, putting my papers and pen down on the opposite side of the conference table.

"You already told him. Do you think he believes you?"

"I think he's trying to believe the best in you and it's his mistake."

She seemed to take that as a triumph. "His decision, right? No one's forcing him. He is *choosing* to be with me, despite everything, and you have to accept it."

"Why are you doing this to him?" I demanded. "You can have any guy you want, I'm sure."

"Why not Zack?" she said. "He's the best guy to settle down with."

"But you're not settling down," I retorted.

Kimmy gave me a lopsided smile. "Why are you so concerned, Jasmine? You've been out of his life for, like, a decade."

"I care," I hissed through my teeth.

"Well, he's not canceling on me, so I guess he believes me more than you."

"Then why are you here?" I said, more harshly than I intended. "Are you here to gloat?"

"I actually came to take back your invitation," she said pointedly, grabbing her bag and standing up. "Zack and I don't need your *negative* influence on our wedding, so you better not be there."

"What if he wants me there?"

The look she gave me then reminded me of Tim's Look of Condescension. I felt like she was staring down a little girl and a lowly employee at the same time. "Jasmine, one day when you have your own wedding, you'll understand. This day is about *me*, and *I* don't want you there. Zack can't really do anything about that."

Kimmy spoke calmly through all of this. It was almost insulting that she didn't even want to break a sweat in dealing with me. I kept wondering what—apart from the obvious—Zack saw in her.

"You know the way out," I said, leaving the waiting room and slamming the door behind me.

THE NEXT MEETING of Zack's exes happened quite spontaneously that night, after Lena and Marjorie got out of yoga class. We met at Chili's.

"I can't believe she went to your office!" Marjorie gasped. "Three hours of restful meditation all gone. I need a drink."

Marjorie asked for the drinks menu. I tried telling them about my dinner with Zack and Kimmy's visit, but it was hard to get the story out in a nutshell.

"What *exactly* did she say?" they kept asking. "What exactly did *you* say?"

Lena and Marjorie do have something in common, I thought as they hounded me further. *They're both obsessed with details.*

A pitcher full of Marjorie's chosen margarita arrived at the table, and she poured a glass for each of us. "I don't get it," she said. "Why is Zack still pushing through with the wedding?"

I shrugged. "And he knows what Kimmy's like."

"You're telling me he just gave up? And has accepted that he's going to put up with her for the rest of his life?"

"That bothers me," Lena said, taking a huge gulp from her glass. "Zack's always been... would you say romantic?"

"Yes," Marjorie agreed. "And optimistic."

"And idealistic," Lena added.

"And *fun*."

"You're talking about him as a boyfriend, right?" I sulked, now a little jealous.

"Is Kimmy pregnant?" Lena asked out of the blue.

I remembered her taut abs, which I noticed in the tight dress she wore six months ago, and then again in the extremely flattering white suit I saw her in earlier. "No," I muttered. "Unless she got pregnant yesterday."

"What hold does she have on him?" Marjorie wondered, frustrated. "And what exactly did you say to him?"

"I said she slept with someone at the conference! That's what you wanted me to say, right?"

"And?"

"He said I shouldn't believe people who want to start rumors about Kimmy because he's supposed to completely trust her."

"Great," Marjorie groaned. "She's turned him totally against me now."

"I've also been uninvited to the wedding," I said. "So I'm not going to object at the last minute, if that's what you're thinking."

"This is bad," Lena sighed, pouring more margarita for herself.

I saw that the lost cause was starting to sink in for Lena. That was the same way I had felt earlier that evening, before I met up with them. I stayed late at work and cried in a bathroom stall—on a different floor, so no one I knew would run into me.

How did I explain what I was feeling?

How about... crushing regret?

Lena's sadness was more of that—sadness. She felt sorry for Zack and wanted to help him. But she could be comforted by the fact that she couldn't really have done anything to change his mind.

Marjorie was angry because she hated the girl who was causing this drama, and also because her credibility was being undermined at the same time. But she had moved on, and she was in a new relationship.

I was the screwed one here. *I* was going to lose him.

Down my throat went the margarita, so fast I didn't even taste it.

"Did you tell him that you love him?" Marjorie asked.

Did I? "No," I said, sheepishly.

"Fuck. What is *wrong* with you, Jasmine?" Marjorie said, tapping me on the shoulder. "You're doing this all wrong. You show up out of nowhere and ask him to leave someone at the altar? And you didn't give him a reason to?"

"Why is this *my* fault?" I yelped, trying to avoid her accusing finger. "I told him about Kimmy's affair."

"Do you need fucking cue cards? He was waiting for you to tell him you love him. And you didn't do that!"

"It's too late," I said, putting my cell phone on the table. "He's not accepting my calls. He won't talk to me."

"So we give up?" Lena asked sadly.

"I'll think of something," Marjorie said. "And you should too, Jasmine. You know him better than we do. You should be able to reach him."

THIRTEEN

I still went to the gym on Saturday mornings.

When I signed up a few years ago, it was because I was dissatisfied with my life and wanted to expel my negative energy. The upside was I magically dropped a size and didn't feel winded anymore when I climbed the stairs.

The gym was just outside my village, near a shopping center I visited if I needed groceries or fast food. When I was in a bad mood, I usually overdosed on my therapies—two hours at the gym and then ice cream at Dairy Queen right after. Just like today.

I assessed my situation—justifying my Oreo Blizzard indulgence.

One, Zack was still not speaking to me.

Two, I was mad at myself for how I handled Kimmy. I decided that I was too civil to her, and I pretty much let her walk all over me.

Three, I almost wished I had never met up with Lena and Marjorie to begin with. I was *fine* two weeks ago. Sure, Zack had stopped seeing me, and his wedding invitation came out of nowhere, but because I didn't know how to feel about it, I shrugged it off and moved on.

Ignorance was bliss.

But not now. Now that Lena and Marjorie sprinkled their unwelcome enlightenment on me, I couldn't just forget about it. My insides hurt at the very thought of Zack marrying *her*—and being out of my life for as long as she was in control.

The other great thing about going to a gym near the village was that I was in my comfort zone.

I wasn't going to run into anyone from work, or anyone I had previously worked with, or Tim who was a Quezon City guy. If I saw anyone there, it would be a neighbor, or maybe an odd familiar face from grade school, or...

"Jasmine?"

... Gerard, Zack's brother, and his wife Ria.

I put my Blizzard down and gave them little awkward hugs, trying not to actually touch skin because I was still sweaty. "Hi!" I greeted, hoping I didn't sound too surprised.

Gerard took a seat in front of me. "Mind if we join you for a few minutes? We need to sit down."

Ria took the chair next to mine. "How are you? How long has it been, Jasmine?"

Gerard did not look much like Zack. Zack had a larger frame, broader shoulders, and darker shades to his hair and skin. Gerard was thin and very pale.

"Too long. I heard you gave birth! Where is Greg?"

"With his *lolo* and *lola*, as usual," Ria grinned.

"We took a break to get something from the grocery. You came from the gym?"

"Yeah." I pointed to the second floor. "It's up there."

I met Gerard and Ria for the first time at Zack's dad's birthday party. It was probably my first month on the job. I had caught a ride home with Zack, and he asked if I wanted to stay for dinner.

"Birthday party for my dad," he said.

For some reason, I thought it would be a loud, noisy party with beer and chicharon and videoke, but was surprised to find it was a small family dinner.

Just Zack's parents, his brother, his brother's new girlfriend Ria, and me.

Oh, wait, beer and chicharon would be my dad's birthday, I thought, giggling to myself.

I was only vaguely familiar with Zack's family, having said hi and hello a few times the entire time we'd been friends. I also stayed for dinner once or twice, but the family wasn't in full attendance, and it wasn't a special occasion.

I remembered how much fun it was. It was like seeing Zack in context—the light and jokey relationship he had with his dad, the slightly competitive one with his older brother, the gentle manner he had toward his mom. I also managed to stay in the background, because they were meeting Ria for the first time that night—so she and Gerard were in the hot seat.

Apart from the wickedly delicious crispy pata served that night, I enjoyed a very civilized interrogation of Ria, all under the guise of getting to know her. Gerard was getting really uncomfortable as the night went on, and Zack didn't let up on his inane questions.

"What's the most expensive restaurant he's taken you to?" Zack asked, addressing Ria directly.

She was a good sport, and played along. "Probably the one in Tagaytay."

"Whoa!" Zack and his dad howled with laughter. Apparently the inside joke was that Gerard was a cheapskate—he never dated because it was too expensive, and even when he did, he still tried to do it on the cheap. Zack explained to me later that because Gerard had spent so much on a date meant that Ria was probably the one.

Five years later and here we were.

"You look great, by the way," Gerard observed.

He seemed like he meant it, and wasn't just being polite. "I lost weight? I have job satisfaction now?"

"How have you been?" Ria asked sincerely.

That was nice of her, because I never really got to know her much, as a consequence of being in and out of Zack's life.

"I'm good," I lied through my teeth. It did get easier the more times you did it.

"Will we be seeing you at the wedding?" Gerard asked.

"I... no," I admitted. "You won't."

Husband and wife caught each other's eye, and that in itself was cryptic. Ria leaned toward me. "You do know he's getting married, right?" she whispered. It was like she was passing on gossip, which I would have found funny any other time. "Did they invite you at all?"

"I was invited. But now I'm not."

Gerard shook his head, looking exasperated. "I can't believe him."

There it was again. The feeling that everyone had already had the conversation before, and *I* was the only one who didn't understand what was going on.

Why are they annoyed at HIM? What exactly did he do?

"I don't understand why he's doing this." Gerard went into Concerned Older Brother mode. "He didn't involve us at all in the wedding—just gave us the invitation and told us to show up."

Ria nodded, trying to remain diplomatic, but she probably felt the same way. "We thought he was going to marry *you*. I thought—finally! And then we read the invite and it was some girl we had never even heard of."

"He never introduced her to you?" I was shocked.

Gerard shook his head. "Not at all. And I was... I mean, we were living in the same house until recently. He was there when Greg was born. He was just acting the way he always was. I didn't know that this was going on all that time. I thought he had gotten back together with you."

We were never together! Even his BROTHER has the wrong idea?

"Do you know what happened?" Gerard asked. "I mean, seriously. One day, you were driving him home and he collapsed on the sofa, and the next, we find out he's marrying this girl."

That's how it was for me too. "He never said anything?"

"Well, we had the baby and then we moved out... it got crazy so we stopped trying to figure it out."

"Mom and Dad have tried to talk to him, but he's not budging," Ria shared. I probably wasn't supposed to know most of this, but they were telling me anyway. "He keeps saying that this is his decision and we should get off his back."

Gerard snapped his fingers. "Do you think you could talk to him? Just ask him if he's really sure? Mom needs to know he'll be okay."

They both looked at me expectantly.

Not again.

"I'll try," I managed to croak out.

I was going to need more ice cream.

FOURTEEN

"Go to room 2805. It's a meeting room. He's waiting there for you."

Marjorie could be her own GPS, I thought, smiling as I read her text message. It really was quite amazing what she could do in a short amount of time. *And that is why she's a hotshot manager and I'm not. Yet.*

Although I had to be given credit for actually coming up with a plan. Or at least, an idea for a plan.

I just wished I didn't have to go through with it.

I headed up twenty-eight floors to the meeting room. Their offices were warmer, homier than mine—the surroundings less angular. There was a lot more wood paneling, and the employees seemed a bit older. I had no problem with the guard on their floor; he let me through after I showed my ID.

I entered the meeting room.

"Hi, Ramon," I said.

He didn't seem to know what he was doing there. "Hey, Jasmine." He stood up to give me a quick hug. "Marjorie told me you were interested in the position on my team?"

"She did?" I marveled again at her ingenuity. If I could pick up some social skills from Lena, I could take some lessons on resourcefulness from Marjorie. "Um, no I'm not. I'm here to ask you about Zack."

I'd like to say Ramon and I went way back, but that would be a bit of an overstatement. It was true that among Zack's friends I knew him the best, but Zack wasn't a guy we bonded over. Mostly, my college memories of him involved an awkward tango and a barely acceptable cha-cha.

But by a certain twist of fate, he ended up in the same office as Zack, so he was the only person I could go to about this.

"I don't know anything," he answered automatically.

"Really? Nothing at all? Sit down, Ramon."

"I don't know what to tell you."

"I haven't even asked you anything."

"Look," Ramon said, sitting down but looking really uncomfortable. "You know how Zack is. He doesn't talk to me about any of his girlfriends. Well, except you maybe."

I rolled my eyes. "Yeah, yeah, whatever. Do you know how he and Kimmy got together?"

"They just suddenly were. Together. I found out that he and Marjorie broke up, and then he started showing up to events with Kimmy."

The poor guy really seemed clueless, but surely he saw something. He probably didn't know what it meant.

"Do you think Zack is happy?" I asked.

Ramon shrugged. "I really don't know. He never says anything."

"Well yeah Zack *never says* anything. I was asking what you think. You've known him longer than anyone here at work."

The look he gave me was hard to decipher, but I recognized it. *He's thought about this before.* Ramon probably didn't want to betray his friend.

I need to ask the right question...

I tried this: "Is he different now?"

"Yes," Ramon said, and I must have gotten it right.

"Different how?"

"He started spending more time with us—when he isn't with Kimmy."

"When, recently?"

"Ever since they got together."

"When did they get together?"

"Last year. I think their wedding is supposed to take place right after their first anniversary."

Before or after he took me to the bed and breakfast in Antipolo? I wondered. *It must have been before. Why didn't he say anything?*

"Why is that different to you? What if he wants to hang out?"

He shook his head. "I can't explain it. But you know him, right? When things are fine, we never see him. He just does his own thing. But when he's like, tense or troubled..."

"He looks for his friends." Yes, I knew this.

"We hung out *a lot* this past year. It's not weird to anyone else but..."

"I understand." Not that it was evidence of anything, though. All Ramon and I had were our hunches, based on atypical behavior from a guy we'd known for almost ten years. But maybe he'd changed? I had, after all. Nine years was enough time for me to come out of my shell.

And then I tried this next: "What's Kimmy like?"

"She's... well, you've seen her."

"Yes I have," I said, bitterly. "She's gorgeous."

"Also very... look, I don't really want to talk about her."

"Why not?"

"She *knows* things. I think she has spies in the office or something. It's a good thing she's on a site visit today."

Marjorie timed this well. "We're in a meeting room. Do you think she has it bugged?"

"I don't mean that, it's just that Kimmy is very *determined*. We never really know what she'll care about, but when she decides on something, she won't stop until she gets it. It's a pain to compete with her for projects, so some of us just drop out when we know she wants it."

I was taken aback. "When did you lose your spine, Ramon?"

He laughed uneasily. "Jasmine, some things aren't worth fighting for. I can let go of a corner office or a business trip to Hong Kong. But I've put my foot down and competed with her over things that actually matter to me. Are you willing to do that?"

"What?"

"Why are you really here, Jasmine?"

"I need your help. Zack won't agree to see me. He won't even answer my calls." I leaned closer to him, in case Kimmy's spies had their ears pressed to the door. "I need to talk to him in private—and she can't be anywhere near."

"That's almost impossible," Ramon said. "She always knows where he is."

"Just set it up, please," I begged. "I need to talk to him. If he insists on marrying her, then I at least tried. But you're right. I'm putting my foot down. This is something that matters."

"I'll try," and Ramon echoed the words and the tone I used to answer Gerard.

Try? We have less than two weeks left! There is no try.

"I actually have an idea," I said reluctantly. "That might make it easier for you."

FIFTEEN

I should have arrived earlier.

Ten days before Zack's wedding, on a Wednesday night, I chose to wear my new jeans.

I should have worn a different top.

The simple white tee looked awkward now, considering what I was about to do.

Not sexy.

The room was at the end of the hall, a corner unit that probably had a view of Manila Bay. I sucked in my breath and rang the bell.

Someone got to the door, and there was a slight delay while I was inspected through the peep hole.

The door opened a crack.

"Are you J?"

"Yes that's me."

The guy at the door, still in a business shirt and tie from work, let me in. "You're not what I expected," he said.

I shrugged. "Well, this is me."

The condo was small, with a kitchen, dining room, and living room squashed together in a small common area. The tightness of the space was somewhat remedied by its multi-functional décor; it looked basic and modular, right out of an IKEA catalogue.

It had a great view of the bay, though.

Only two guys were in there, similarly dressed.

"Where's Ramon?" I asked.

They were looking at me—then at each other—eyes darting back and forth regularly like a tennis match.

"He'll be here in fifteen minutes," the other guy said.

Still with the crazy looking. I totally understood why, but it was making me uncomfortable.

"Can I just stay in the bedroom?" I suggested, although it wasn't exactly a request.

"Sure," the first guy said, snapping out of his trance. "This way."

We walked past one door (probably the bathroom), and toward the second door on the other side of the space.

"Do you want something to drink?"

"No thanks," I said abruptly. And then I remembered that I was supposed to at least be nice. "Just let me know when Ramon arrives."

He looked like he wanted to say something else so I closed the door and cut him off.

The bedroom itself was simple, in a nice way. The lights had dimmers, and I played with them for a second before keeping them at a soft glow. I sat down on the double bed and checked my watch.

Almost ten.

The sheets felt clean, at least. They probably rented the condo because it didn't look like it was lived in. Something colorful on the nightstand next to the bed caught my eye, even in the dim light.

Condoms. Lots of them, in sealed foil packages. Taken

out of their boxes (I assumed they were purchased in boxes), and then scattered in bunches on the table. Different colors, sizes, flavors.

I groaned. *So this is what happens at a bachelor party.*

I locked the door in case one of Zack's office friends decided to try anything funny.

I HEARD people start to arrive. Male voices talking loudly over the TV, offering each other beer and pulutan.

The guest of honor wasn't around yet. The snippets of conversation that flitted underneath the door were about work. They all seemed to be Zack's officemates.

Apparently, a bachelor party was an absolute NO according to Kimmy, Ramon had said. She had already anticipated that the guys would plan one and had told everyone that it was *not* going to happen.

"But you guys are still doing something behind her back, right?" I had asked.

Ramon had buckled, looking and maybe feeling like a snitch. "Yes. On Wednesday night. Kimmy's assigned to Laguna and we were going to bring Zack to this condo we got."

"Then that's perfect."

"No it's not."

"You've got to get me in there, Ramon."

"But..." And the look on his face was priceless. "The guys are expecting a stripper."

"Zack doesn't know but *everyone* is expecting a stripper?"

He shrugged. "Zack doesn't know it's his turn, but it's

not our first time doing this. Everyone knows what this is. I'm sure even he's expecting it."

"If this doesn't work, go to a strip club after. I'll pay for it. But you *have* to do this for me. I will owe you."

Turned out, Ramon was a nice guy. He took charge of the sneaky bachelor party, told the guys he had found a stripper, and arranged to bring Zack to the condo.

Easy, right?

Where is he? This was taking a lot more than fifteen minutes. My hands were getting cold and numb. I think I sat on them and unwittingly cut off my own circulation, and jumped every time I heard the front door open and close.

Still no Zack.

Then, a text message: *On our way up.*

I didn't hear the door this time, but the cheers that erupted in the room made it clear who had arrived.

Another text message: *Someone's still talking to him. Stay there. We'll hang out here first. Then I'll send him to the bedroom.*

I put my face in my hands. I could hear my heart pounding in my ears, and I swore I could even see it beating through my shirt. *Shit, Jasmine, what did you get yourself into?*

IT SOUNDED like Zack didn't want to go into the bedroom.

"Just send her out here!" someone drunkenly yelled, annoyed at the delay.

"No," I heard Ramon say firmly. "She's here for Zack."

"Boring," one guy said.

"At least show us *something* first!" went another guy. "He doesn't even want it!"

"Kimmy will kill him if he tries anything!"

"Are you kidding? Kimmy will kill all of us!"

"Screw Kimmy! You're all pussies."

God how pathetic.

Text message: *Did you lock the door? Unlock it.*

"Seriously, Ramon, it's okay. I'll pass." That was Zack's voice, and it was nearer than all the others. Ramon had probably brought him all the way to the door, but he was hesitating.

"I don't care, Zack. Trust me what's inside the room is not what you think it is. Anyway I'm throwing you in there and do your thing and don't come out until you're done."

I crept up to the door and unlocked it.

Ramon swung the door open and pushed Zack inside, slamming it shut behind him.

Zack looked disoriented by the dim lights. I got to the knob before he did, squeezing between his body and the door, locking it before he could pull it open and escape.

"What the hell?" His eyes were still adjusting to the darkness.

"Hi," I said quietly, still pressed between him and the door. "I think we should talk."

SIXTEEN

Surprisingly, or maybe not, the sound of people being lightly slammed against a door didn't bother any of the guys outside. Or maybe they didn't hear it above the sound of their own partying.

Zack stepped back slowly. "Is this a joke?"

"Kind of," I said. "I'm supposed to be the stripper."

"Oh. *Oh.*" He eventually backed into the bed and sat on it. Then he started to laugh. "Oh, God. It's been a weird day."

Not the reaction I was looking for. "Are you okay?"

"Yes, yes, I..." Zack dropped his head into his hands, and kept it there for what seemed like a really long time. His shoulders shook softly. I couldn't tell if he was laughing or—

Crying? I stepped toward him, tentatively.

He straightened up, shaking his head. "I'm fine, I'm fine."

Not crying. But he looked tired. Even the flattering dim lights didn't hide his bloodshot eyes.

That wasn't the way an excited groom-to-be was supposed to look, right?

I might have a chance. I dropped to the floor in front of him. "Can we talk now?"

It took a while for his eyes to fix on me. First they scanned the room, taking in the bed, the window, the locked door, the condoms on the nightstand...

"What are you even doing here?" he asked flatly.

"You wouldn't agree to meet me."

"So you decide to crash my bachelor party?"

"Would you have met me? Even if I begged?"

"No," Zack confessed. "I wouldn't have."

"Why not?"

"What did you want to talk about?"

I couldn't believe he was still trying to be evasive. "Zack, you're stuck here. Those guys outside think you're with a stripper. You might as well tell me everything."

"Jas," he said, extending the "s" like a sigh, "I don't know where to start."

Don't be confrontational. Don't make it about you.

I summed up all my maturity and tried to think of what to say. Marjorie wanted me to give him a reason to leave Kimmy, but I couldn't just spring that on him. *Not if he actually loves her. I have to look out for his happiness first. Right?*

"Do you love her?" I was afraid of his answer.

Long pause. "She's all right."

I was relieved, and offended, at the same time. "That is the stupidest thing I've ever heard you say. Why didn't you tell your family about her? Why didn't you tell *me?* "

"I was going to," he said, a tad defensive. "But then you broke up with Tim, and I couldn't."

"For months, you couldn't mention her at all? Not even to your brother?"

"This isn't about my brother or anyone else."

I probably shouldn't have mentioned that, because I could see Zack's privacy issues start to kick in.

"What's he doing talking about me behind my back?"

"Well you can't exactly blame him. He's worried about you. Everyone I know is worried about you. I don't understand. We were fine months ago, and then you disappeared."

"We made a deal," he said, so softly that I barely heard it.

"You what?"

"Kimmy and I. We had a deal. She would stop her habits, and I would stop seeing you."

I didn't need *another* reason to hate her. "Why would she ask you to do that? She doesn't even know me!"

"Please, get off the floor. That's got to be uncomfortable."

"No," I started to say, but that moment wasn't the time to be defiant. I let him pull me up, and sat beside him on the bed. The soft mattress dipped under our weight.

He didn't let go of my hand. The feel of his fingers tentatively finding comfortable positions in mine distracted me.

It's hard to describe what it was like, being that close to him for the first time. There was Zack—and then there was my imaginary ex Zack, the one I'd already kissed and touched and been various kinds of intimate with. It was like the real and pretend were merging, and I wasn't exactly sure what was happening.

"She asked you to stop seeing me? Forever?" I whispered. He was so close.

"Yes. I thought she was being unreasonable. You should at least be at our wedding. You got an invitation." His hand found its place against my palm and pushed forward, fingers interlacing.

"Which was taken back a few days ago," I reminded him.

"I know. It was my idea."

"You sent Kimmy to my office to disinvite me from your wedding?"

"I didn't know how she was going to do it, but I couldn't have you there. I wouldn't be able to go through with it if you were."

"Zack, this is messed up. If you still aren't sure about marrying her, why did you ask her in the first place?" I couldn't wrap my head around what he was saying.

His hand gripped mine fiercely. "I didn't want to wait for you anymore."

"But I'm just here," I said softly, frowning.

"Yes, but never—" His voice started to trail off, and he didn't continue. "It doesn't matter now." Zack was shutting down, as he always did when anything private was brought up.

Well I wasn't going to let it happen now. "But what?" I demanded.

"But nothing. It doesn't matter."

"The hell it doesn't!" I cried. "Is this my fault? What did I do? When was I ever not there for you?"

"You were always there, Jas, I didn't say you weren't!" he protested.

"Then say what you mean, Zachary, I'm fucking tired of guessing."

"Shit, Jasmine. I didn't think you were this dense," he said, frustrated. "I've been waiting for you to fall in love with me for a long time. But six months ago, I finally gave up."

"Why did you give up?" My voice came out small, not indignant—but my heart pounded loudly against my chest.

"You were apart from that ex of yours for months and you didn't respond to anything I did. I didn't want to be your rebound guy. I was there, and didn't push. I thought I'd wait until you were ready. Then I figured that you were never going to see me any other way."

He's right. My brain was all fired up, memories triggered by the simplest word. I had never thought of Zack as anything more, because I never thought he wanted to be anything more to me.

But that argument went around in circles.

He wanted me. I wanted him.

The truth was hard to get used to.

"You never said anything," I said, in my defense.

There was no need for me to be defensive, because he wasn't angry. He seemed way past anger and was instead closer to acceptance. "I didn't want to ruin it. I guess you were the closest thing I had to a best friend."

"I don't have anyone else either," I told him.

"I didn't want to scare you off."

"Why didn't you think I felt the same way?"

"Because you...you just let me be with other people. You didn't care who I dated."

"You *chose* to be with them! I wasn't going to get in your way! You let me stay with Tim for three years!"

"Are you *kidding* me? Is that how you remember it?" He didn't raise his voice at me, but the bile hurt. "I hated that guy from the start and I never lied about it. I let *you* stay with him because you kept choosing to go back. Even when I was there the whole time."

"Don't put this on me! You were with another girl the

entire time that was happening! And you didn't even tell me about Kimmy!"

"Kimmy and I were just going out," Zack said. "I didn't intend to let it get this far."

What a fucking understatement. "Wow, that's a surprise. Because suddenly getting a wedding invitation? That's taking it too far. That really, really hurt."

"I didn't hear you protest when you got it."

"Did you want me to? Were you trying to provoke me?"

"Yes," he said slowly, as if realizing something for the first time. And then, more pointedly: "Yes. Deep down, I guess I was hoping for a reaction—anything—from you. But I didn't get anything. Kimmy isn't as bad as people think she is. I would have made it work if I had to."

"Well, this is my reaction. It's delayed, but you're getting it. You're a *jerk*." My hand balled into a fist and I aimed it pitifully at his chest. "When I got that invitation? I wanted to tear it to shreds. And shove it down your throat. I hated that you were getting married, *hated* that I didn't even know who she was until that night, *hated* that you didn't even bother to tell me yourself. I thought it was a good thing you disappeared from my life because I would *kill* you the next time I saw you."

Hitting him—however limply—was strangely cathartic. The huge knot (nerves? tears? pain?) that had formed in my chest started to loosen, and I had to hold back my hand to keep from doing it again.

"But now I know why I hated you so much then. I didn't realize it before but now I know," I said quietly. "Zack, I love you."

He blinked at me. And then swore in several languages, pushing himself off the bed. "Jasmine, you better not be playing me."

"I just opened up my soul to you and that's what you say?!"

"You don't know how much I've wanted to hear you tell me that."

I grabbed his hand and pulled him closer. Standing, he towered above me. "I love you."

I didn't realize how much I had hurt him, all those years of not knowing how he felt. My hands tightened around his, but he was adamantly—defensively—unresponsive.

Except his eyes, which were boring into mine, pleading. "Don't joke about this, Jasmine. I'm about to cross a line here. Don't say something now that you'll want to take back tomorrow."

"I love you, Zack." I repeated, with more conviction.

His mouth captured mine in a kiss. It was not at all gentle—it was forceful, hungry, the kind of kiss that had been waiting nine years to happen.

How we ended up on the bed is a matter of debate. I remember grabbing handfuls of his shirt and pulling him down, falling back on the bed. He remembers lunging at me, and that he had gotten the white tee over my head even as we landed on the center of the mattress. He claims that I should have been kinder to his shirt instead of ripping it off. I maintain that if I could have been kinder that night it would have been to his upper back, which I may have dug my fingers into a little too deeply.

His tongue and hands had their own agenda, exploring my collarbone, the hollow of my neck, my breasts, the curve of my waist. His breath on my skin alone trumped anything we had made up in our canon—this was real, and I felt stupid for having relied on a made-up version for so long.

His scent was embarrassingly familiar—I remembered all the times I met him right after he had showered, every time I sat next to him in the car, every friendly embrace we shared. How could I have ignored it then, and yet couldn't seem to get enough now? I hungrily pressed my lips to the skin on his shoulders. His hands gently caressed my face, then I started to float back to reality when I realized that he was talking to me.

"....sex with Tim?" he was saying.

"Don't stop," I managed to stammer.

"I said, did you ever have sex with him?"

"I don't think that we should be talking about—"

"I just need to know if you've done this before."

"Shit, you should have asked. Yes. Does it matter?"

"I need to know how gentle I should be."

I snapped out of my stupor and rolled my eyes. "We've been waiting for this for nine years, Zachary. How gentle do *you* think you should be?"

He laughed. "Finally, we're on the same page about something."

I sank back into the bed, waiting as he picked one from the pile and did the responsible thing. Light from outside helped me see him, finally, see the various changes that the years had done on his body. All good things. My fingers were drawn to him; I reached forward and touched his abs, traced up and around a rib. "What was our first time like, Zack?"

"You mean the one that isn't now?"

"Yeah."

"It was perfect." He dropped to his elbows, bare skin on mine. The touch was cool for just long enough for us to both gasp, and then it felt warm, and warmer. "It was perfect. It was the first time for both of us but it wasn't awkward at all. I made you come twenty times. You said you were never going to want to do it with anyone else."

"Wow." I started giggling. "That's great. I'm so happy for imaginary me."

"You think I would have given you anything less? I'm the best version of myself in our canon, Jas."

No, he was already the best as himself. I mean, he wasn't perfect, and I wasn't perfect, and it was obvious that no perfect person would ever get into this mess we had made. But I understood him.

And he loved me.

For a second there I stopped giggling, and began to understand what was happening. This was real, for once. This was almost a decade of something and it was *true* now. Our eyes met, and I knew he was thinking the same thing. And he thrust into me, finally, and it was our first time. A real first time. We were catching up to the relationship we had created and it felt *great*, like finally everything made sense.

His hips moved, and I challenged his pace. And wow he was right, it wasn't awkward. It was desperate, it was all tingly tension, everything I craved for and in the best way. Why did we wait to do this? It was perfect pressure, perfect timing, bodies communicating what we needed. Responding, giving. I couldn't get enough. I came as he pressed kisses against my face, then again with my cheek against the sheets. I was above him, when *his* release caught up with him. My hands were in his hair. I felt it happen to him, here, and now.

All of it was real.

SEVENTEEN

I woke up to the following text messages.

Ramon: *I don't know what's happening. We'll be here another hour.*

Ramon: *The guys are getting restless. I'll take them out in thirty minutes.*

Ramon: *You can stay there until four PM. Then I have to pay for an extra night. Text me.*

Lena: *Is everything okay?*

Marjorie: *Well?*

It was ten thirty-four AM.

"Shit," I cursed under my breath, firing off a quick "*not feeling well, staying home today, please ask Marian to take charge of applicants today I'm sorry I'm sorry*" to my boss.

The covers stirred, and Zack's head emerged from underneath a pillow. He had a happy smile on his face.

"Good morning," I grinned. "You look..."

"Rested?"

I tilted my head. "I was going to say younger."

"I feel both right now, thank you. I slept very well. How are you?"

I touched my face. "Oily."

"I was going to say you look worried. What's wrong?"

I showed him the time. "It's Thursday. We have work."

"Right. Okay." He reached over the bed for his pants and checked his pockets. "I think my phone's outside. But Ramon will cover for me."

"He's a good friend," I said.

"Did he have anything to do with last night?"

"Maybe seventy percent."

"I should thank him." He dropped his pants back on the floor and curved his arm around my waist, pulling me back to bed. I rolled with him onto my side and laughed as I got tangled in the blanket.

I *knew* how he looked in the morning. Bed hair, sleepy eyes. The morning-after awkwardness wasn't there.

"It really does feel like we've done this before," I said, planting a kiss on his chin.

"Well yes. In my mind we have. In many different ways."

I rolled him onto his back and kissed his neck, underneath his Adam's apple.

"When did you know you felt this way about me?" he asked.

His throat made curiously wonderful vibrations against my lips. "Years," I said.

"You're retconning."

"You're not asking the right question. I've known for years that you were always going to be part of my life. That I'll always care about you. That it would be nice if I actually found out what it was like to kiss you, and everything else. I knew that. Even if it seemed impossible because of the other people who were around. But two weeks ago was when I decided to do something about it."

"Seriously?"

"Yeah. With the help of some fairy godmothers."

Last night was a risk that wasn't easy to take, but in a few hours I was repeatedly reminded how glad I was that I took it. He shifted on top of me. Unlike last night, the room was flooded with light, and he looked at me without saying a word. Long enough to make my toes curl back, self-conscious.

"I'm actually happy that we just did this now," he smiled. "I'm sorry if last night it sounded like I wished it had been sooner."

"We did waste a lot of time."

"But I would have been different."

"I don't think you're different. You're still my Zack from college."

"I *am* different," he insisted. "I don't know if I'm any better or worse, but I would have probably lost you if we had gotten together earlier. I made some bad decisions in college. Hell, even after."

"Well, you did base your first relationship on a lie."

"See? You would have left me before we even graduated."

"So you think Lena was right? About her first girlfriend theory?"

"I didn't do very well with my second or third girlfriend either."

"Let's not tell Lena." Might as well keep that a secret too.

"You're different too, Jas." Zack's finger lazily traced a path from my forehead to the tip of my nose. "You went from this girl who avoided everyone to someone confident. Passionate. Sexy."

"Yes, the college Jas was definitely not any of those things."

"But I fell in love with you anyway. And I still love you now. I've always loved you."

"You told me." I smiled at the memory. "Last night. Several times."

Then his mood changed. "I have to talk to Kimmy," he said, his tone somber.

I sighed. I knew reality was going to find us eventually. "You're calling off the wedding, right?"

He looked at me, somewhat horrified. "Yes." Duh. "But she's not going to take it well."

EIGHTEEN

As I was having dinner with my family, I got a generic text message from Zack: *Sorry but wedding's been cancelled. We will return your gifts.*

As soon as I got that, my phone started ringing.

First call was Gerard, Zack's brother. "Did you have anything to do with that?"

"Yes," I said, and that probably came off a bit mysterious. I heard Ria's excited voice in the background. "Are you and Zack back together?"

"We were never—" *Why bother?* "Yes. Yes, we are back together."

"Mom will be so relieved!" I could hear Gerard's grin in his voice.

I ended the call and my phone rang again. It was Marjorie.

"I heard! My work friends got the text! I didn't get it 'cause I wasn't invited but they forwarded it to me and I've been trying to call you the past five minutes!"

"Does Lena know?"

"Yes! I forwarded the text to her. Are you two back together?"

"Yes."

"That is fantastic! I've been hearing all these weird rumors. Anyway! We'll meet up and you'll tell us everything!"

Not everything. "Yes, Marjorie, we should!"

The next call was Zack.

"Hey," I said, excusing myself from the dinner table and taking the call in my bedroom. "Everyone's been calling me."

"Me too. They're asking me what the hell happened with the stripper," he said, laughing.

"How did it go with Kimmy?"

"She knows. That's all that matters."

I had a sinking feeling we hadn't heard the last from her.

I DIDN'T HAVE to wait very long.

I was at a coffee shop when I felt someone lurking behind me.

I picked up my no-whip mocha and turned around. It was Kimmy. She looked like she had just come from work—phone in her hand, bag tucked under one arm. How did she find me, when I had walked into this particular coffee shop almost at random? Was she following me? She did have eyes everywhere.

"I told you to stay away from him," she said sharply.

I walked out of the coffee shop with her at my heels. I just made it out the door when she grabbed my arm. "Hey! I'm not done yet."

"What do you want, Kimmy?" I asked, shaking her off me. "It's *over*. You know that. I'm sure you saw it coming."

"He wanted to be with me," she said, gritting her perfect teeth. "No one leaves me like that."

"Kimmy," I began. "I don't know you very well, but I hope you eventually see that this is the best for everyone."

She laughed scornfully. "Right. You both wasted my time, my money, and *humiliated me* in front of everyone."

"It's not personal." She wasn't going to believe it, but I needed to say it. "I'm sorry, but even you have to know that this wasn't the right thing to do. You obviously don't want to be tied down."

"You don't know what I need or want," Kimmy said. "And he wanted to be with me. At least until you showed up again."

Please realize that we set your manipulative, cheating self free. And let's move on.

When she talked again, her voice was softer but still unkind. "You have no idea how painful this is."

"I'm sorry," I said sincerely, not knowing what else to say. "I really am."

She turned on her heel and walked away.

My phone vibrated in my pocket. A text message from Tim: *I heard.*

I rolled my eyes and texted back: *Get over it.*

NINETEEN

I thanked Ramon by taking him to dinner. "Thanks. I really owe you. More than this dinner."

He smiled. "I'm glad my instinct was right. Zack looks happy. And I haven't seen him at all since last week."

"Has Kimmy been bothering you?" I frowned.

"I think she's only started to figure out my role in the whole thing," he said. "But don't worry about it. Marjorie's got my back at work."

Next, I debriefed Lena and Marjorie over dinner that weekend, on the day the wedding was supposed to have taken place. They were both happy for me, although I suspected that Marjorie was happier because of her complicated feelings about Kimmy.

"Does Zack know that we approached you about this?" Lena asked.

"Yes," I answered, "but he's not ready to see all of us together at the same time. The very idea of this freaks him out."

"I especially love the way you stood up to Kimmy." At

this, Marjorie poured each of us a glass of wine, extra cheerfully. "She deserves to lose at something once in a while."

"I don't know. She seemed really affected by it. Maybe we should leave her alone and let her sort it out."

Marjorie was not as forgiving. "We did her a favor. She should be thanking us!"

"I propose a toast," Lena said, lifting her wine glass. "To first love. And true love."

"And self-awareness," Marjorie added.

"And meddlesome exes," I said.

"I'll drink to that!" Marjorie was unable to contain her glee.

When Zack picked me up, after killing time at the gym, he made sure that we were done with dinner.

I ran a hand through his hair—damp from a shower—and kissed him. "How was the gym?"

"Relaxing."

"You showered."

"I always shower when I have to drive you home."

"I'm still working out what's real and what we made up. But you're absolutely right. And hey, next time, you should at least say hi to the girls."

I could have sworn I saw him shudder. "Sorry, no. I can't do it. I hope you eventually stop telling each other stories about me."

"Hey, I never told them that we were never together to begin with. I'm good at keeping secrets!"

The great thing was, we could finally let the secret go. It was real now, and we could start over.

No more imaginary exes.

"I heard the funniest thing at work today," Zack said as we pulled into the highway. "Rumor has it that I left Kimmy for the stripper at my bachelor party."

"And you told them the truth, right? *Right?*"

He laughed. "Not exactly. It's a good story! And much simpler than the real one. Maybe we should add that to the canon."

And that is why, if you ask any of our friends, you wouldn't be able to get the proper story of how Zack and I ended up together. No single person—apart from the two of us—knows exactly how it happened.

Which was exactly how he wanted it. He was, in many ways, still my Zack from college.

The End

AUTHOR'S NOTE, 2017 EDITION

I love this book. I'm proud of it. It's the first one I wrote that was published, I wrote it relatively quickly, and I managed to keep track of all the timelines. I'm almost glad I didn't stop to ask myself why craft it this way...I just ran with it. Some risks pay off.

When I wrote this, I was figuring out the kind of author I wanted to be, and how to write "chick lit" in English. I made decisions that have stayed with me years later, like writing mostly in English, using recognizable Manila settings. My characters would be sexually active, and responsibly so.

This 2017 edition is different from the first published edition in several ways, because *some* decisions I wanted to correct. Or adjust. I'd like to discuss some of those updates here.

- If you have any of the previous editions, and enjoyed the book, the story hasn't changed, okay? But we had to trim several thousand words the first time, and as I went through this again I feel I was able to add back more context. More context, dialogue, and backstory should help make certain things clearer.

- I edited how I described the physical appearance of characters. Some specific descriptions remain, but to be consistent with how I write now, I removed a lot of what I no longer feel is necessary or proper.
- If a thing no longer exists, or the term for it has changed, I removed it or updated it.
- I extended the sex scene. Because I write those now. (I didn't before.) Thank you, Marian Tee, for telling me to do this.
- And then, the most substantial edit: someone in this book calls Kimmy Domingo a bitch, and I removed that. I edited how other women talked about Kimmy, but tried not to alter Kimmy as she was. In this book she's the villain, and that can't be helped—that's what the premise called for. I kept as much of her personality and her volatile relationships intact because it will matter, all of it, in the book where she's the main character (Love Your Frenemies, Chic Manila #4). In my mind, she always had that backstory, and the events parallel to the version depicted here were always clear to me. I knew where she was coming from. That meant *I* understood Kimmy, but I wrote her using the limited POV of people who didn't, and that led to some readers hating her. I've since decided to not be this kind of author, as much as possible. I've since tried to "make it up" to Kimmy by writing a full book about her, keeping her

character and actions from this book consistent, and not watered down for sympathy.

Thank you for giving this book, and me, a chance. Thank you for the friendships that came into my life because of it.

By the way, Zack and Jasmine are happy right now. And forever.

Mina

CHIC MANILA SERIES BY MINA V. ESGUERRA

Contemporary romances set in the Philippines. Can be read as standalones.

My Imaginary Ex (#1), Jasmine and Zack
Fairy Tale Fail (#2), Ellie and Lucas
No Strings Attached (#3), Carla and Dante
Love Your Frenemies (#4), Kimmy and Manolo
That Kind of Guy (#5), Julie and Anton
Welcome to Envy Park (#6), Moira and Ethan
What You Wanted (#7), Andrea and Damon
Iris After the Incident (#8), Iris and Gio
Better At Weddings Than You (#9), Daphne and Aaron

PREVIEW: LOVE YOUR FRENEMIES

Tuesday

Dress fitting
Hair and makeup trial
Despedida de Soltera at Tita Chat's

The message from my best friend Chesca was simple and direct: *You better be here by Tuesday lunch OR I WILL KILL YOU*.

I got that not from the original email, but through the chain of people she had copied, in case I insisted on ignoring her. Still, it was Tuesday morning, and I was indeed back in Manila.

My mother did not know I was arriving that day. For months now I had only been communicating with her through courtesy texts informing her which country or city I was in. She tried to call, but I only talked to her once, and just to tell her that roaming was expensive and she should just email me if she needed to speak to me.

That was mean of me, because I thought she would never figure out how to email. She did, but I still didn't reply.

The airport taxi dropped me off and I managed to make it to the stairs before she saw me.

"Kimberly! I swear you are going to give me a heart attack." She put down her cigarette and gave me a hug.

Like many females I can name, I had a complicated relationship with my mother. It was better now that I was twenty-seven years old, and only because we both accepted some truths about each other: That I was no longer as immature as she thought me to be, and she was not as mature as I wanted her to be.

"You didn't know I was arriving today?" I asked cautiously. Sure, she acted surprised that I was there, but Mrs. Erica Domingo was known for being dramatic every now and then.

She pressed a kiss on my cheek. "Honey, I know you're supposed to be here today, but I said I wouldn't believe it until I saw you in my house. How are you? Are you back for good this time?"

"Yes, my savings has been officially drained," I said. "I'm back home now." For better or worse.

People hated me. I don't feel bad about it anymore. Everything is so relative.

Depending on the day and person you asked, I was *rude* or *manipulative* or *heartless* and other more colorful words. To the point that, when my fiancé told me that he was in love with someone else—nine days before our wedding—a bunch of people actually thought, great, Kimberly Domingo was *finally* getting punished.

How could that even happen, right? How could you get that close to a wedding and see it fall apart?

Like with most disasters, once you stepped back and really thought about it, you'd realize that it wasn't caused by just one thing.

First, there was the whirlwind romance. The time frame from first date to wedding date was a year, a short engagement.

Second, the groom-to-be had just gotten out of a relationship of several years, and though he was a great guy there were many things he hadn't worked out yet, things that came to a head embarrassingly close to our big day.

Third and maybe the most telling, the bride-to-be was me, and I was a bit of a mess.

Those who wanted to see Kimberly Domingo get hers had a lot of good stuff to choose from in the weeks and months that followed my non-wedding.

It started when I found out—through a call in the early afternoon, to my personal phone, which I had taken while sitting at my workstation. It wasn't an office with a door, and my cubicle walls looked and felt like plastic reinforced by a layer of thin carpet. Yeah, no soundproofing when I started raising my voice.

"You're kidding me, right?" I tried to whisper, but as my former fiancé firmly explained to me that the wedding wouldn't be happening, my voice started to get loud and shrill. "*What about the caterer?*"

"We won't get our deposit back, but at least we haven't paid them in full yet."

"But my lola's already on her way!" Eighty-five years old and as we were speaking, flying in from California.

"I'm really sorry, Kimmy. But we really can't do this."

"You know what we can do? We can just shut up for a second and think about this. What happened?"

He was calm as he explained to me what his decision was, and what needed to be done. He had an answer for everything I threw at him: he was prepared to call all the companies we had booked to announce the cancellation, as well as all the guests, and was even offering to pay for a few things that I had advanced from my own account. And that I would have the money by Monday.

"Shit, Zack, I don't fucking care about the money right now! What the hell happened?"

I can't remember exactly what he said. I was in a rage, and when the phone call ended I was suddenly aware that I was in my place of work, and everyone probably heard that.

I don't remember the rest of that day. My mother told me that I came home late, but by then she already knew, because Zack had contacted her with his apologies. I have a vague memory of not wanting to go to work the next day. I remember crying into her lap, wiping tears onto the floral-patterned fabric of her nightgown, first with loud, angry sobs, and then hiccupping like a child. I had never felt like that before, ever.

Humiliated. That was the word.

It was hard to go to work after that. No one said anything to my face, of course, but come on. This was an office, just like any other within the tall buildings along Ayala Avenue. It was full of people who liked to talk about other people, and in my case, with some schadenfreude. I worked at a large consumer goods company, and as an upstart management trainee was under more pressure—and given more visibility—than the average employee. Even just the rumor of wedding troubles would have been enough to earn me the top spot in all office gossip conversations, but with the scene I caused, screaming at my cellphone? I guaranteed it.

My mother told me it would get better, and eventually the office started gossiping about someone else. But I lost something, and every time I worked with someone I wondered if they respected me less. Some people at least had the benefit of hitting rock bottom in private.

The last straw was when I showed up at a meeting, months after the incident, to discover that the brief I had prepared for all participants lacked one sheet of paper. I had forgotten to print it out.

My boss at the time, not exactly the nicest person either, made a big deal out of it for fifteen minutes. While he ranted to the eight executives sitting around that conference table—also to the two regional officers on conference call with us in Shanghai and Sydney—I sat back and took it, my nails digging into the leather upholstery of my swivel chair.

"I think it's because you didn't take a break, Kimberly," he said. "I've let your mistakes the past few months slide, but this is such an amateur mistake. You've been letting your personal life get in the way of your work."

I don't need this. My side of the story? The project we were presenting was crap, and I had unwittingly given my boss a way to blame me for everything. That missing page wasn't that big of a mistake, but parading it around in front of everyone—and making it seem like I was an emotional wreck—was undoing all the years of hard work I put in.

I excused myself from the meeting, headed to HR, and told them I was quitting. As soon as I could, I found a flight to LA.

Some people think I didn't do the right thing then, that leaving was cowardly. *I* thought so too. I had been dreading this trip back, but I knew I'd have to deal with it eventually.

What I hadn't told my mother yet was that though I was back "for good," I was planning to move out of the home I had shared with her all my life.

Estranged from my dad and sister, I lived with her in a large house in a gated community in south Metro Manila. The house was too big for us when we were a complete family; in the years since the separation it became, as far as I was concerned, a two-bedroom townhouse with three large storage rooms. And yet, not much about our routine changed: the same kind of breakfast was served every morning, the same dinner plates showed up when we had company over, my laundry basket disappeared at the same time every few days and my clothes showed up neatly pressed and folded the same way.

It became clear to me then that so much of what I knew of my life at home was determined by my mother, and she tried to make me feel like nothing had changed. I appreciated that.

What did change was that we never really saw my dad's side of the family again. But it wasn't like I hung out with my mom's family anyway—I only saw them during awkward, official gatherings like weddings and funerals, and it was that way since I was sixteen years old. My mom was a complicated woman who burned a lot of bridges; the only people who could stand her were her best friends from high school. These women, and their families, became the only family I really knew.

So it wasn't such a big deal, that thing I did. I quit my job, went to the US, and wasn't seen for a year. My mom was first to master the art of disappearing on family. What I did was tame, and shocked only the casual observers.

Taking off was harder than I thought it would be. Not the concept of it, but the execution.

When I was younger I heard stories of teenagers who would run away. In my high school, I think a girl tried to do it. While it sounded easy in theory, I wasn't sure what she was trying to accomplish. How exactly was she going to get money? How many bags of clothes could she bring? Where was she going to stay, and how long could she stay there before someone tipped off her parents and sent her back? And, what bothered me most—what if her parents didn't want her back?

On this topic Mom was the surprisingly reliable source of information. She didn't blink when I told her that I managed to get an MNL-LAX-MNL out of what would have been two honeymoon tickets to Seoul. When I complained about not being able to pack light, she peered at my luggage critically. It was large enough to fit a human being.

"How long will you be away?" she asked.

I shrugged. "My return trip's in six months."

"You won't be spending Christmas here?"

I didn't think of that. "I guess not."

Christmas wasn't *that* big of a deal for my mother, I quickly told myself. I could remember a few Christmases in my teens when she wasn't around, either because she was on a cruise with my dad (in happier times) or with friends.

She didn't make a big deal out of it. Instead, she started picking things out of my bag. It formed a small pile on the corner of my bed. No heavy winter clothes. Just a few pairs of pants, a simple skirt, a nice dress, tops in various earth colors, a sweater, some night shirts and underwear.

"That's all you need," she said when she was done. "Anything else, you buy when you need it, or borrow. Do you have enough money?"

"I think I have enough." Despite losing money on the wedding, I had enough saved up to live on, very simply, for a while.

"It's never going to be enough. Call these people and stay with them if you're going to be around." She wrote names and numbers on a piece of paper—her trusted cousin in San Francisco, a close friend in Illinois, a former business partner in Florida. "You know what to do when you run out."

What went unsaid there was "*Ask your dad*" who was still our silent benefactor for when things went to shit. I never asked him for anything, but I suspected that he bailed us out a few times over the years.

At LAX they decided to indeed give me six months in the US, and indeed the money was never enough. But at least there was novelty, and being in unfamiliar places, encountering strange and different things every day, was a healthy distraction for the most part.

On this "sabbatical" I learned something too. I learned why my mom liked to take off. It cleared the mind, so it focused only on what mattered. I discovered what just might keep me sane when I made my way back to Manila, and the first step was to move out of my mother's house.

So now that I was finally home, what kind of reaction did I think she would have? I wasn't just away for six months, as we had originally talked about. Instead of going back to Manila, I arranged to stay in Hong Kong instead, hopping around a few more countries in southeast Asia (visas not required), and then settling with a friend in Singapore for what would have been the longest stretch right before I came home.

"Put your dirty clothes in your laundry basket. It's still in your room," she said, no big deal, like I had come from a weekend trip.

I heard a car drive up to the house, and familiar footsteps going up the steps to our front door. I shot a panicked look at her.

She shrugged at me. "Don't look at me, dear, I'm just as surprised as you are." A moment later and she made a stealthy exit, up the stairs to her bedroom.

I contemplated running up to join her, but he was already in the house.

I didn't even hear the door, and in the next moment he was standing there in the middle of the living room. He looked different somehow—dark hair a little longer, skin suntanned instead of his daily *mestizo*, shoulders broader than I remembered. My heart did a little leap; the old physical responses to his presence were still there. Hated that.

"You're home," Manolo said.

It was a dance that I still knew the steps to.

He would walk into my space. His right hand would reach for my left forearm, lightly touching the inside of my elbow. His left hand would go up to the curve of my neck, thumb gently on my throat. His right arm would pull, the fingers of his left hand would nudge, and my hands would go up to cradle his jaw, leading his mouth to mine.

The first time, I sort of just ungracefully fell into the kiss, as I guess most fifteen-year-olds would. Over the years our personalities changed, we got more practice, and then I not so much *fell* as *took* a kiss from his mouth as if I was collecting what was mine. I knew he felt the same way.

ABOUT THE AUTHOR

Mina V. Esguerra writes contemporary romance, young adult, and new adult novellas. Visit her website minavesguerra.com for more about her books, talks, and events.

When not writing romance, she is president of communications firm Bronze Age Media, development communication consultant, indie publisher, professional editor, wife, and mother. She created the workshop series "Author at Once" for writers and publishers, and #romanceclass for aspiring romance writers. Her young adult/fantasy trilogy Interim Goddess of Love is a college love story featuring gods from Philippine mythology. Her contemporary romance novellas won the Filipino Readers' Choice awards for Chick Lit in 2012 (Fairy Tale Fail) and 2013 (That Kind of Guy).

She has a bachelor's degree in Communication and a master's degree in Development Communication.

Addison Hill series: Falling Hard | Fallen Again | Learning to Fall

Breathe Rockstar Romance series: Playing Autumn | Tempting Victoria | Kissing Day (short story)

Chic Manila series: My Imaginary Ex | Fairy Tale Fail | No Strings Attached | Love Your Frenemies | That Kind of Guy | Welcome to Envy Park | Wedding Night Stand (short story) | What You Wanted | Iris After the Incident | Better At Weddings Than You

Scambitious series: Young and Scambitious | Properly Scandalous | Shiny and Shameless | Greedy and Gullible

Interim Goddess of Love series: Interim Goddess of Love | Queen of the Clueless | Icon of the Indecisive | Gifted Little Creatures (short story) | Freshman Girl and Junior Guy (short story)

The Future Chosen

Anthology contributions: Say That Things Change (New Adult Quick Reads 1) | Kids These Days: Stories from Luna East Arts Academy Volume 1 | Sola Musica: Love Notes from a Festival | Make My Wish Come True | Summer Feels

Contact Mina

minavesguerra.com
minavesguerra@gmail.com

BOOKS BY FILIPINO AUTHORS
#ROMANCECLASS

Visit romanceclassbooks.com to read more romance/contemporary/YA by Filipino authors.

CPSIA information can be obtained
at www.ICGtesting.com
Printed in the USA
FSHW011630040621
82102FS